SKAGWAY

It's All About The Gold

BRENDA WILBEE

Brenda Wilbee

Stewart Goodfellow Publishing

SG

Brenda Wilbee

Nonfiction narrative of Skagway, Alaska's, history and highlights, offering an expanded (but concise) history of Skagway as the "Gateway to the Klondike," portal for the 1897-1898 Gold Rush stampeders. Narrative accompanied by gold rush photographs and sketches by the author.

ISBN: 0943777143
Library of Congress: 2013940902

Cover Design:	Brenda Wilbee
Interior Design:	Brenda Wilbee
Front Cover Images:	• "Snow Storm on White Pass Summit" Courtesy of the University of Washington Libraries, Special Collections, HEGG 197
	• Skagway's Arctic Brotherhood Hall Courtesy of Blake Kent: VictorPhotography.org
Back Cover Image:	• the Author Courtesy of Blake Kent: VictorPhotography.org
Photo Sources:	Library of Congress Alaska State Library University of Washington Special Collections Blake Kent, VictorPhotography.org Brenda Wilbee

All sketches are done by the author, © 2013

Stewart Goodfellow Publishing

Seattle, Washington
Brenda@BrendaWilbee.com
Printed in the United States of America

to
Blake

thank you

other books by Brenda

Brenda Wilbee

Skagway: It's All About The Gold

From The Author

The summer of 2010, my son, a seasonal Skagway, Alaska, bus driver and tour guide, thought I might like being a garden guide at Skagway's Jewell Gardens. An avid gardener and ready for adventure, I fell in behind Blake and followed him north.

I first lived in an old cabin without facilities and then a remodeled meat locker, brushing my teeth in a communal bathroom while the accountant peed in a urinal two feet away. I was pushing sixty; this was a stretch. But being a Canadian by birth and loyalty, an American by circumstance and choice, the interconnection of common gold rush history between the two countries made me feel oddly at home.

Before the summer was out I went to work for Alaska Excursions as well, handily enough next door to the Garden. I split my days in the office, on the docks, and amongst the delphiniums and Lady's Mantle. Each day was different. I loved the mystery. The anticipation. So much so I returned for the 2011 Season, this time following directly in my son's footsteps as a bus driver for HollandAmerica-Princess. I wanted to take visitors not only around town and through the Garden but up into the Yukon—where grizzlies roam, where porcupines rattle and scuttle out of the way, where gold once made people honest-to-God crazy. The following season, 2012, I went for the gold itself, Dawson City, Yukon— destination point for the 1897 Klondikers of more than a century ago. There, I drove tourists out to the discovery claims where all this craziness began.

In my real life I'm a writer. Seven of my novels are biographical, so I'm this odd amalgamation of writer, historian, and tour guide; and

Brenda Wilbee

I set out to write a series of books Skagway visitors could take home, books that would offer an expanded (but concise) narrative of the history and an enhancement of everything they saw in the Gold Rush corridor—specifically it's early days, the town, and the trail north. *Skagway: It's All About the Gold* is the first.

Research, of course, doesn't occur in a vacuum. I am dependent upon those who go before me—and rely heavily on Tappen Adney (a Gold Rush reporter), Pierre Berton (Canada's foremost Gold Rush historian), Jefferson Randolph Smith II (Soapy Smith's great-grandson), Catherine Holder Spude, PhD (former NPS employee), and the many first-person accounts uncovered in the vertical files of the Klondike Gold Rush National Historical Park's archives. To Adney, Berton, Smith, Spude, and a bunch of dead people, then, I owe a debt of gratitude.

That's the research. When it comes to the writing, many have aided:

• Ginny Cochran, Skagway friend—for befriending me from the start and whose hospitality ran the gamut from tea and cookies to a roof over my head.

• Stanley (Beth) Knouff, roommate—for her love, joy, enthusiasm, forbearance, and contagious goodwill, pulling me always toward the adventure.

• Shari Guida, down-the-hall friend—for making me laugh and providing, at the last minute, the missing book!

• Jess Callies, Mark Walker, Nolan Jahn, Nick Mistretta, Juan Casteneda-Gonzales, Amy Perkins, Dave Ferrier, and Eric Bernardi, all Jewell Garden friends—for their collective *jois de vie* that keep Skagway summers light and happy!

• Blake Kent, son—for obvious reasons. By the way, if you'd like color prints or digital copies of his Alaska and Yukon photography, they can be purchased for reasonable rates through VictorPhotography.org.

• Heather Williams and Phil Kent, daughter and son—for their hands-on help in the Lower 48. The seasonal life is more complicated than one might think. I've needed their love and support more than I care to admit.

• Dallas Williams and Katie Kent, son-in-law and daughter-in-law—for the same.

Skagway: It's All About The Gold

• Bruce Wiggins, my brother-in-law and owner of U.S. Printing—for printing this book!

• AC, a good friend and colleague—for downloading his music and movies onto my laptop, allowing me happy respite while wintering in Skagway.

• Skagway Public Library—for everything!

• Karl Guerke, Head Historian of the Klondike Gold Rush National Historical Park—for his interest, answers, conversation, and review of my work.

• The many historical archives in Washington, Alaska, BC, and Yukon—for their gracious access to all things historical.

• Ruth Craig, Judy Mallory, Sue Deramo, Cindy Godbey, Tim Saulter, Bee Lingle, Betsy Aldecker, Mike Anceravige, Les Kellogg, Steve Caulfield (Lep), John McDermott, Karen Dunford, Miranda Massey, Helene Crouch, Jen Castle, Rin Clark, Nadine Lockette, Billie Clem, Deb Beucher, Maggie Boughton, Skipper Stovall, and Nils Davis, residential Skagway friends—for their friendship and unique contributions to this project.

• Finally, Wayne Schroeter, high school BFF—for his friendship, generosity, and wisdom, enabling me to winter in Skagway the winter of 2012/2013. *Je t'aime et merci, mon bon amie.*

For all things Skagway, go to my blog at SkagwayEtc.blogspot.com.

Brenda Wilbee

Skagway: It's All About The Gold

Table of Contents

Brenda Wilbee

Skagway: It's All About The Gold

Preface

"You know a man's crazy, George, if he prefers fishing with the Siwash when there's gold lying about."

George Washington Carmack, a tall, laid-back Californian who wanted nothing more in life than to be a "Siwash" (and having done the next best thing by marrying a Tagish princess) paused in his work to greet Bob Henderson, a handsome man from Nova Scotia—a man who'd obsessively been looking for gold since he was fourteen years old, a man with Australia under his boots, Colorado, and now the Yukon of Canada's Far North. He'd just paddled ashore at the First Nation's summer fishing village nested along the Klondike River mouth where it flowed into the 2,300-mile Yukon River. A pile of gutted salmon lay in a slippery stack between the two men as Bob approached—men about as different as they could be: Bob, intense, serious-minded, chiselled features; George, sleepy-eyed, softer through the chin, a ready smile and easy laughter. His Tagish wife, Kate, kept to the task at hand, stretching salmon onto a drying rack, though occasionally she had to drive off the dogs. Her nephew, Charley, sat on his haunches, keeping a steady rhythm of snagging salmon from a bucket, slicing and scooping—offal going to the dog pack, fish to the silvery, slippery pile. Other buckets—brimful of fish fresh from the river—awaited attention. George said to Bob, "And where would that gold be? Lying about, you say?"

"Up at a creek I've called Gold Bottom. Eight cents a pan, but you better hurry. Me and my boys took out $750 in three months. A lot of folk from Forty-Mile'll be headed that way."

Brenda Wilbee

George Washington Carmack, better known as Siwash George for his preferred lifestyle, knew several native dialects and wore his mustache First Nation's style—the Oriental handlebar dropping just below his chin. He rubbed his hands on a pair of filthy jeans and gazed into the distance. His brother-in-law Skookum Jim, Kate's brother, approached from the river where a net had been strung across its width to catch the annual salmon run. A Herculean force of a man, supremely handsome, Jim set down a couple of baskets with fish still flopping around and listened in. He may have been Tagish, but he wanted nothing more than to be a white man. What better way than to find a lot of gold?

George said, "You know I'd rather make a dollar fishing salmon, Bob, than chasing after rainbows. Going to make dog food out of this. And then there's logging. Forty Mile needs timber. And I had that dream, you know."

Bob shook his head. He knew about that dream. Everyone *knew about that dream. Siwash George had dreamed of finding a salmon with gold nugget scales and eyes made from $20 gold coins. He'd interpreted the dream to mean he ought to keep on fishing.* Crazy. *George really* had *turned native.*

Skookum Jim chimed in; eight cents a pan was good money. Bob cut him short. His opinion of the First Nations was, as he liked to boast, low on the totem pole. "George, if you hurry, you might stand a chance, but I don't want no damn Siwash staking a claim along Gold Bottom."

Jim sucked in his breath. Charley broke rhythm. Kate stiffened. Oblivious to what turned out to be the biggest mistake of his life, Bob paddled off—but not without suggesting George pay him a visit or head up Rabbit Creek not far away, to where he'd earlier spotted some gold. "If you come across anything better than eight cents a pan," Bob called off his shoulder, "let me know!"

This is *what you did in the Yukon. You let everyone know—unlike in the States where, if you found gold, you kept it a secret, worked it as long as you could, then shot to kill. Still, George was hard pressed to drum up any sort of promise when he waved Bob goodbye. The comment had stung. He, Jim, and George—and Kate of course— were family.*

Skagway: It's All About The Gold

Skookum Jim sourly commented in the pidgin Chinook so common in the Yukon, "What's matter dat white man? Him killet Inchen moose, Inchen caribou. Ketchet gold Inchen country. But him no liket Inchen staket claim? Wha for?" *Loosely translated,* What the hell?

"Never mind, Jim," said George, and then tweaking Kate's pretty cheek, he said, *"You'll just have to find your own creek."*

Which is what Jim did a few days later. They'd gone to see Bob— where one more time the man had insulted Skookum Jim, refusing to sell him a plug of tobacco—and were coming back down Rabbit Creek when Jim shot a moose. The three men—Jim, George, and Charley—decided to camp out so they could dress the meat for Kate back at the Klondike River mouth; and in the morning Skookum Jim woke, went to the creek for a drink of water, and found a nugget the size of his thumb.

They told everyone but Bob.

Brenda Wilbee

Too Windy For The Sane

Before the Klondike Gold Rush of 1897, no one lived in Skagway of Southeast Alaska. The natives thought it tantamount to insanity.

The term "Shghaghwei" or "Skagua" is native. To fully translate would require an entire English paragraph, but its essence is "wind." A personal favorite is "air you don't breathe twice." In winter, it comes stinging like a whip out of the north, down off the Coastal Mountains at fifty and sixty miles an hour. During the summer it's the opposite, funneling up the valley with enough force to just about peel bark off a tree. The local Tlingit,* specifically the Chilkoot tribe, preferred the sheltered inlet of Dyea* four miles NNW as the raven flies and situated at the foot of their ancestral trail where, for at least two centuries, they monopolized all coastal trade with the Interior—a trail they aggressively guarded.

Coastal Mountains and "Skagua" In 1895
Library of Congress: USZ62-122304

---

*   Kling'-kit
*   Dy-ee'

Brenda Wilbee

The Chilkoot Tlingit, however, were not unfamiliar with "Skagua." Half a dozen fox and bear deadfall traps were found in the valley during the mid-1880s, and a native family living at Smuggler's Cove once trapped both sides of the river. But no one ever thought to settle the windy area, leaving a forest of spruce and hemlock, cottonwood, pine and birch to endure. The discovery of gold in the Far North changed everything.

Speculation

Twenty years before the big gold was found in 1896, a growing number of prospectors had been slipping into the Far North, panning for gold along the lacy rivers and streams of Canada's Yukon—and were beginning to realize an average of $2,000 a year. Canada, ever mindful of lawless Americans spilling into British Territory the minute any real gold might be found, sent up her Dominion Surveyor in 1887 to define the international border. Border established, Canada could then send in the Mounties as preemptive strike against American mayhem. But Canada wasn't the only one thinking of gold in the Yukon and what it might mean. Captain William Moore had been following gold all the way up the continental spine.

Born in Hanover, Germany, in 1822, Bill Moore was only seven years old when he first sailed before the mast. His sea roving eventually took him to New Orleans where, at twenty-two years old, he became a Mississippi River pilot and married Hendrika. Two years later, in 1848, he fought in the Mexican War and was, at the end of his service, awarded American citizenship. The two-year-old reports of gold in the California Sierras sent him West in 1851. Two years, however, too late.

CAPTAIN WM. MOORE, 1896
by the author/from a photograph

2

Skagway: It's All About The Gold

He vowed to never again be late for a gold rush. He never was.

Hendrika and their growing family followed him for the next thirty years—Peru to Alaska. He made and lost at least three fortunes in gold by building and operating schooners, steamships, constructing trails under government contract, getting miners to and from the latest gold discovery, and prospecting himself. Vigorous, courageous, competitive in his battle for dominance in the Pacific Northwest freighting business and with a nose for gold, he was by 1886—*ten years before the eventual gold strike*—a legend. Sixty-four years old that year, he sent sons Billy and Ben up to the Yukon to investigate what he knew in his bones would be the "next big thing."

A year later, 1887, he was again bankrupt, his fleet of steamships and family mansion in Victoria, BC, Canada, up for auction to satisfy debts. But his reputation for boat building and river navigation, coupled with his inside knowledge of the Far North, to say nothing of his legendary veracity and know-how, attracted the interest of none other than Canada's Dominion Surveyor William Ogilvie, who, in the spring of 1887, was in Victoria putting together his team for the boundary survey.

Captain Moore still had the easy gait of a man half his age—just the sort who, with his knowledge, could easily build Ogilvie a scow on the other side of the Chilkoot Pass in SE Alaska and effortlessly navigate the surveying party from Lake Bennett to the Yukon River headwaters...and, finally, navigate them another 400 miles down the rapid-riddled Yukon River to Forty Mile, government seat, where Ogilvie would set up headquarters. Was Captain Moore interested?

A flurry of gold had just been found near Forty Mile and his sons were in the thick of it. He had in his pocket a letter from Billy Jr. telling him that while the gold looked promising, the really *good* news was of a "secret" trail not far from the Chilkoot. An Interior Tagish man by the name of Skookum Jim had shared the information. A rarely used trail, with a lower pass, maybe, thought Billy Jr., it could be developed to accommodate pack animals? As soon as the really big gold was found, this secondary, ungaurded trail might be an advantage—because the only way to get a horse up and over the Chilkoot was on its side, roped, and hauled.

So *was* Captain Moore interested in joining the survey team?

3

Brenda Wilbee

He might have been sixty-five in 1887, but Bill Moore's instinct for making money and sniffing out the gold was undiminished. Whenever the big gold in the Yukon was found and it would be—perhaps tomorrow, perhaps in ten years, who knew—the quickest, cheapest way to the Interior would be through these two passes of SE Alaska. This new "*secret*" pass, as of yet under no one's control, held enormous potential for a man mired in bankruptcy. He said yes to Ogilvie.

The party left Victoria on May 13, 1887. Eleven days later, in the wee hours before dawn, the *Ancon* steamed into Lynn Canal—a gigantic trench of water in the Alaskan hinterlands, described by historian Roy Minter as being "created by some prehistoric upheaval that left in its wake a narrow ribbon of water stretching eighty miles..." At dawn, the *Ancon* put into Haines, the ship's northernmost port. At eleven, it dipped its flag and blew its whistle and left Moore and Ogilvie *et al* standing on the wharf in the pouring rain, needing to transfer seven tons of gear into two Petersborough canoes to be towed another twenty miles north in the miserable weather, to the very end of Lynn Canal—Dyea.

There, they were greeted by John J. Healy. A Montana man, he'd started Healy & Wilson Trading Post at the foot of the Chilkoot Trail in Dyea the year before, brokering furs for the natives and outfitting the steady trickle of miners heading north. The place was unimpressive. A few clapboard houses, a log hut, maybe two—a native village tucked along wet woods, sentinel to the trail.

Healy knew nothing of a second trail. Nor did the 138 natives living in the village. Yet Skookum Jim, the very fellow who'd spilled the beans to Captain Moore's son, was there. "I hunted up Skookum Jim when we arrived," the captain later reported. But the First Nations on the north side of the mountains were far more passive than their aggressive coastal cousins on the coast, adverse to cross them. Centuries of harassment and intimidation had given them good reason and Skookum Jim, pressed by Moore, disavowed all knowledge. Moore had to give it up. More important things pressed. Ogilvie was having trouble with the Chilkoot packers.

They'd taken one look at his canoes and seven tons of provisions, assorted equipment, a prized camera and were refusing to haul for anything for less than $20 per hundred pounds. "These Indians are

continued on p. 7

4

— JOHN J. HEALY —

℞

John Jerome Healy hailed from the Canadian/American West. Working out of Montana, he ran the nefarious Fort Whoop Up in what is now Alberta, Canada, near present day Lethbridge. His whisky (watered down with red pepper, ink, Jamaican ginger, tobacco, and black strap molasses) was decimating the Blackfoot. To establish law and order and protect the First Nations people, the Canadian government formulated the now famous Northwest Mounted Police in 1873 to drive Healy and the other traders back across the border. Their primary target, Fort Whoop Up—and Healy.

When the Mounties arrived after a six-month trek in 1874, their collective resolve sharpened by an epic journey of deprivation and hardship, they expected one heck of a fight. All they got was Dave Akers—a fur trapper the fleeing Healy had left in charge.

"Been expecting you," said Akers, "supper's on."

The irony is that years later Healy made his way to Dyea, Alaska, and also the Yukon, partnering in 1892 with big money in Chicago. He, among others, wrote Ottawa asking for police protection from the growing American lawlessness in the Canadian Yukon. One more time the Mounties showed up. Not to run Healy out, but to protect him.

HEALY AND WILSON, DYEA 1898
Library of Congress USZ62-50199

—KEISH / SKOOKUM JIM MASON—

ＣＲ

Keishe was born near Carcoss, Yukon, in 1855, son of an Interior Tagish mother and Coastal Tlingit father. No one knows when or how he acquired the name Jim Mason, but Skookum is Chinook for strong. He was that.

A story not well known is told by Captain Moore's son Ben. In 1891, they were in Ben's schooner, along with a mutual friend, when Jim spotted two bears along the shoreline and asked to be let out and go hunt them. They off-loaded Jim's canoe and Jim dropped down into it. Rifle and four cartridges in hand, he set off.

SKOOKUM JIM MASON
by the author/from a photograph

"I'll wait an hour!" An hour later, Ben went to investigate — and came across a bloody Jim, hands, face, clothes badly torn.

"What happened?"

The bears had retreated up the mountain. Rather than risk shooting at long range Jim had followed them almost to the snow line, killed the black and wounded the grizzly.

"So where's the grizzly?" Ben asked.

"Down hill in bushes, but not dead yet." Jim pointed and told a tale of hand-to-hand battle — showing claw marks on his hands from ramming his gun into the bear's throat and striking him on the head with heavy stones.

With some difficulty, the three men got the black bear loaded into the schooner, then picked up a few more cartridges and went to finish off the grizzly. As they approached, Ben could hear great noises of snorting and moaning, bushes crackling, swaying. Quietly Jim leaned forward, parted the bushes, took aim, and fired.

"I was surprised to see such a large bear," wrote Ben. "Both it and the black one had beautiful coats. Jim showed me places on the bear's head where he had bruised him with rocks and slashed him with his knife."

Eventually, by rolling, dragging, and lifting the carcass over rocks and boulders, they got the grizzly aboard the schooner. Jim sold the skins to Johnny Healy for $40.

"This was a cheap price," wrote Ben. "Johnny Healy wasn't in Alaska for his health."

perfectly heartless," Ogilvie fumed years later in a memoir. Capitalism was the last thing *any* white man expected and Ogilvie was annoyed. Finally, a compromise was reached: $10 per hundred pounds—but only to the summit. The Interior Tagish would take over the final miles to Lake Bennett for another fee—an arrangement carefully negotiated by Healy.

They got underway June 6th with just about everyone in town hired to tote and haul. Only the elderly and infants were left behind. The first few miles, wrote Ogilvie, were over a "stony moraine of glacier." Then it was "up a steep pass, climbing more than 3,000 feet in six or seven miles, some of it so steep that the hands have to be used to assist one up, a stiff test of strength and endurance."

THE CHILKOOT TRAIL: DYEA TO LAKE BENNETT
by the Author

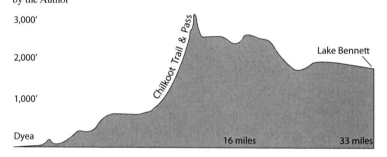

Here Skookum Jim proved his sobriquet (skookum meaning strong) by hauling 156 pounds of bacon on his back in one trip. As to when he let slip that he *did* know of the pass, no one knows. Bullish by nature, tenacious, Moore had undoubtedly been persistent. But they'd have to go back to Dyea, Jim said, and canoe over to "Skagua" Bay, then zigzag up the mountains from there. Moore broached the subject with Ogilvie—who was, by that time, more than happy to give the men leave. A trail unencumbered by the capitalistic Chilkoot was worth pursuing. They'd meet in a week, he told Moore, at Lake Bennett.

The captain and Jim backtracked and canoed five miles SSE out of Dyea, passed a cove and rounded a bluff into "Skagua"—the windy inlet no one wanted to live in. A forboding place. Driftwood on the flats, clumps of coarse grass waving from the shoreline. A dark forest

mantled a narrow valley and on either side—to the east, to the west—
high mountains rose straight up into mist and fog. In the distance,
Moore could see masses of blue-white glacial ice and miles of fractured peaks and ridges. Somewhere in there, the new pass.

It was seven days of a very hard go. Dense underbrush, plunging
canyons, rocky bluffs, tormenting mosquitoes, swollen streams, brush
that slashed their clothes, ripped their skin. The two men scrabbled up
and over boulders and ascended perilous cliffs and crept along break-
away bluffs high above "Skagua" River as it rollicked and tumbled to
the sea. But when they reached the summit, a narrow gash in the rock,
Moore gleefully discerned the pass to be at least 600 feet lower than
the Chilkoot. And the trail, although tough, was suitable enough for
horses. Too, "Skagua" Bay appeared deep enough at high tide to accommodate large ships, a huge win over Dyea's two-mile tide flats, a serious
obstacle that would necessitate tricky off-loading and a scurry to get all
supplies out of the tide's reach.

A new kind of Eldorado was forming in his mind. Instead of digging for gold, he'd build a town, a sawmill, a wharf. When the gold
was found, hundreds, maybe thousands, would need gear and provisions, everything more or less passing through this bottleneck and his
pockets. He'd build a road, charge a toll...

He and Jim clambered through the narrow gash of rock—land
standing on end—and emerged from the pass onto a broad upland of
fractured and crushed granite left behind after the last ice age. A cha-
otic, awesome landscape, interlaced with a plethora of summit lakes
that ran for miles. These they skirted and cut twelve miles northwest
through a boreal forest to where the Chilkoot Trail ended at Lake Bennett
and Ogilvie waited.

Pleased with the news, Ogilvie incorporated Moore's findings into
his own and, because Canada's Minister of the Interior, Thomas White,
had authorized the survey, Ogilvie named "White Pass" after him.

Signs of boat building were fully evident along Bennett Lake—
tree stumps, sawdust, abandoned whipsaw platforms. Prospectors
were coming up in greater numbers than Moore had expected. The
new pass, lower at the summit... Surely, this would be the preferred
trail. But why stop at a trail? he thought, a road? *Why not a railroad?*

Skagway: It's All About The Gold

"Every night during the two months he remained with us," Ogilvie later wrote, Moore pictured "the tons of yellow dust yet to be found in the Yukon Valley. He decided...that Skagway would be the entry point to the golden fields...and the White Pass would reverberate with the tumble of railway trains carrying supplies." Sugar plums surely danced in the old man's head while he felled a few trees, whipsawed them into lumber, framed in a twenty-foot scow, and spiked on the boards!

July 11th they were underway. But for Moore it was the wrong direction. He wanted to go south. He wanted to stake his claim and petition the government for permits. Call on favors, beg loans. So no one was too surprised when one mosquito-infested morning—camped along the Yukon River and spotting young Ben Moore poling upriver from Forty Mile on his way back to Dyea and the Outside—the old man joyfully greeted his youngest boy, "rolled his blankets aboard, and bid Gov. Ogilvie adieu."

Moore must have talked his youngest son Ben into the new venture because they went straight from Dyea to Juneau, purchased tools and provisions, and paddled back up to the lonely, windswept "Skagua" beach in a canoe so heavily laden it rode just six inches above water at midships. They arrived October 20, 1887. In the silent, lonely isolation, surely they took a moment to contemplate the enormity of what they were doing. *A town in this godforsaken, windy wilderness?*

A GODFORSAKEN WILDERNESS
by the Author/from a photograph

Brenda Wilbee

They didn't ponder long. "We ran our canoe up in the creek about a quarter of a mile," Ben wrote, "then put up our tent and camped at the foot of a little bluff on the beach." Even as he struck ax to tree, his father declared, "Here we will cast our future lots and try to hew out our fortune."

Accordingly, they staked their claim (160 acres), filed the papers (Juneau), built their sawmill (primitive), put in a wharf (65 feet), petitioned to build a toll road through the pass (denied), started clearing the trail, built bridges, constructed a couple of log cabins, platted a town site, named it Mooresville. For ten years they came and went, Ben doing much of the physical labor, the captain talking to investors.

Ten years later, July 29th, 1897, the mail steamer *Queen* put in with 200 miners bound for the Klondike River, a tributary of the Yukon—with news Moore had known would come. *Gold! The richest strike in history!*

Finder's Keepers

Who found the gold in August of 1896? For a long time American George Carmack and Canadian Bob Henderson argued. George was the guy on scene—and it was he who filed the Discovery Claim. Reason would suggest it be him. Bob, however, insisted that he'd been the one to *tell* Carmack where to find the gold; therefore he, Bob, was the real discoverer. A petty but important distinction because at the time Canada provided a life-long, monthly pension of $200 to anyone making a gold discovery. The average wage was $5 a day, so this was a distinction worth winning. Bob took his argument to court and Canada—no doubt influenced by Bob's Canadian citizenship over George's American— awarded Bob the title of "Co-Discoverer." Not that George cared. He had the pension *and* the gold. Finder's keepers.

The truth is that neither Bob nor George discovered the gold. It was Skookum Jim and we have the same old story—white guys getting all the credit. In reality, Skookum Jim, the same man who'd shown Captain William Moore the secondary trail out of SE Alaska to the Yukon ten years earlier, had been the one to find the nugget that set the world afire.

This is how it happened. After insulting Skookum Jim at the Klondike River mouth (where Jim, his sister Kate, nephew Charley,

10

and brother-in-law George were all camped to dry fish), Bob started up the Klondike River for a little stream he'd named Gold Bottom, and where he'd been taking out eight cents a pan. He'd paddled a few strokes, then hollered off his shoulder at George, asking him to come up to Gold Bottom for a look-see, and suggested George take a look at Rabbit Creek en route.

Been there, done that, thought George, long tired of the fruitless search for gold. A white guy, he really only wanted to be native. Jim, though, wanted to be white—gold would make him that. So the three men set out with mixed feelings to see what Bob might have upriver.

They were not impressed—not with Gold Bottom, not with Bob. He'd insulted Jim again. Upon being asked to sell some tobacco, Bob pretty much told Jim to go to hell, that no damn Siwash was going to get any of his smokes. Enough already. Jim, Charley, and George headed up Solomon's Dome for the return trek.

A hard go. Their clothes came away in ribbons, lacerated by wild roses, raspberries, and devil's club. After crossing the summit, they stumbled down Rabbit Creek toward the Klondike and home. Late that afternoon they passed a small tributary; another three miles, Jim shot a

THE DISCOVERY CLAIM TODAY, RABBIT CREEK (NOW BONANZA)
Author photograph

moose. They decided to stop and dress the meat for Kate back at the fishing camp. What they didn't know when they laid down that night, atop of two feet of moss, was that they were sleeping on millions and millions and millions *and* millions of dollars' worth of gold. Unaware, and in the morning, Jim went down to Rabbit Creek for a drink of water and wash a dish—and found the famous nugget that set off the gold rush.

Their future unfurled with a snap! A single pan brought in $7—$700 in today's prices. George, who only wanted to be native, no longer did. And Jim, still wishing to be a rich white man, was at least rich. And if today any doubts who really found the gold, the Tagish Nation and Parks Canada both give it to Jim.

The Word Gets Out

Not until the following summer—July of 1897—did word get out. Two weeks before the *Queen* put into "Mooresville" carrying the first stampeders, sixty-eight "Klondikers" had put into Seattle and San Francisco with two tons of gold—over ten million dollars in today's currency. The world, suffering global economic devastation from the Panics of 1893 and '96, sat up. Such news was flint to despair. Optimism ignited. More than a million people around the globe schemed of ways to get to the Yukon. Men, women, entire families were aflame for Canada's Far North and the Klondike River—where Skookum Jim had found the nugget, the size of his thumb. Captain Moore's ship, literally, had come in.

Except the ship was bound for Dyea. Hastily, Ben sweet-talked Captain Carroll into depositing the men at Moore Wharf, and before the hour was out, 200 prospectors were tumbling onto the pier, alive with the latest news sweeping the globe like wildfire. *Nuggets the size of hickory nuts! Scattered like pebbles alongside the creek beds! Thick as cheese in a sandwich!*

No sooner had the *Queen* cast off than the *Islander* followed, then the *City of Mexico,* the *George W. Elder,* the *Willamette*, the *Whitelaw.* Men by the hundreds, women by the dozens, children by the handful spilled into Mooresville and swarmed the beach. Ship captains unwilling to wait for the tide to turn simply dropped everyone and their cargo onto lighters (flat bottomed scows) to be poled through the shallow tide flats and beached. Horses, dogs, cattle, all were dumped in a cacophony to swim ashore. Cargo, piled in hapless disarray, toppled. Everywhere urgency prevailed. *Hurry!*

Hurry before thousands bottle-necked the passes! *Hurry* before the early winter set in—*hurry* before the Yukon River froze, before they were locked out, before the gold was gone! *Hurry!*

Overnight a lonely beach of just two cabins and a sawmill was overrun. John Muir compared the frenzy to "a nest of ants taken into a strange country and stirred up by a stick."

A bewildering sight. Unorganized goods in mountainous heaps all over the beach, bundled hay, tethered horses, single and in teams, great crowds. Men in boots splashed through the water toward loaded skiffs to tote to safety sacks and crates and all sorts of paraphernalia. Others drove wagons right into the swirling tide to take aboard bigger items. Everywhere men hollered their price, called out names, argued and cussed, and yapping dogs got in the way. Along the shoreline men squatted before tents, cooking beans over sheet-iron stoves, and the

MOORESVILLE, AUGUST 1897
University of Washington Libraries, Special Collections: A. Curtis 46104

smell of bacon fat sizzling in the flame wove like a thread through the tapestry of sweat and sea air, and dung. Behind them, the semblance of a mud sticky street riddled with stumps boasted more tents. Four saloons vied for attention with apropos names like Pack Train, Bonanza, Grotta, and Nugget. A blacksmith's shop had you at $5 a shoe, a restaurant advertised by tossing a pair of britches over a clothesline, MEALS painted on its seat. The sound of rasping saws, axes, and hammers tattooed the air, wooden shacks beginning to go up; and painted signs, angled at a tilt, pushed by the wind, informed which were grocers, suppliers, or druggists. Somewhere a gambling house bled music through the open flap of its canvas walls. Convivial gab ran through the encampment like scales rippling over a piano, punctuated by loud bangs of discord—men settling in. Money was to be made on the incoming tsunami and many of the prospectors decided Moore had the better idea: mine the miners. They chopped down the trees heedless to his property rights. They divvied up his land, drove in their stakes, and threw up their tents against the terrible wind. For all his experience on the gold rush frontier, Captain Moore could not have prepared for the lawlessness that came in with the tide.

His wharf manager served notice five days after the *Queen* disgorged the first wave of miners, announcing that no one was permitted to build without appropriate payment. The men simply thumbed their noses at Mr. Hill and went on. A fellow by the name of Dave McKinney, flanked by others, went one step further: He and the others decided to plat their own city. The Moores objected. "Mooresville" had already been platted, properly filed. But their complaint was run up a flagpole of indifference and left to flap in the wind. Frank Reid, surveyor, school teacher, Indian fighter, now bar tender at the Klondike Saloon, a mere tent on the corner of Fifth and Broadway, helped himself to some surveying instruments left behind in pledge for unpaid bills, and drew up an illegal plat of a town everyone called *Skagway*.

United States Commissioner John U. Smith recorded each lot at $5 a pop, corner lots prime, and when these corner lots ran out, an amended plat was filed, equally illegal. The corner lots suddenly became mid-block, stuck at the alleys, and the outwitted claim jumpers quickly joined the Moores in making objection. Their outrage was

Skagway: It's All About The Gold

COMMISSIONER JOHN U. SMITH'S OFFICE, 1897
Sketch by Author, from an illustration

equally ignored and on it went until hundreds of tents — stores, restaurants, brothels, offices, hotels, saloons, and gambling houses — lined the muddy, stumpy streets, morphing one by one into sheds, shacks, and hastily constructed buildings.

Insult to injury, the final plat put Captain Moore's bunkhouse home in the middle of an intersection. Ordered to move it, Moore refused. When a committee showed up a year later meaning business, he seized a crowbar and, wife crying in the doorway, "slugged the man nearest to him, ripping off his trousers with the first swing." Butcher John Laumeister would later recoup the cost of his torn jeans by charging Moore an extra $6 on his meat bill.

Moore paid the bill and, in the end, acquiesced on the house. He and his wife and daughter temporarily moved into Hotel Moore on the southeast corner of the disputed intersection: And his alliance with a British-backed investment company (A&NWTT), brokered one year before the hordes arrived, filed for redress in the courts.

For a time this halted any further attempt to usurp the Moores' property but, less than a month later, close to 100 merchants, including Dave McKinney and Frank Reid, held a citizens' meeting and formed the Committee of 101 to hire J. G. Price to represent them in an aggressive lawsuit against Ben Moore and his A&NWTT Co., the British investment company that managed the Moores' property development. The very next day, October 10, 1897, U.S. Commissioner John U. Smith began again to record city lot claims, taking in his $5 fee, a sum everyone felt unscrupulously excessive. Where wind and forest once reigned, greed now ruled, leaving Captain Moore and son Ben to wonder what had hit them.

Show Us The Gold!

Perhaps the greed can be explained by global economic disaster. Ignatius Donnelly wrote in *The Representative* on August 29, 1894:

> The spectacle of men fighting for work...My God! This is terrible! Battling for the privilege of working all day for enough to eat—and the next day go at it again; and so on until the earth rattles on their pine boxes.

The gold strike came at a time when the world was staggering from global depression, the first economic punch delivered by the failure of Argentina's Baring Brothers late in 1892. The first smackdown in the U.S. happened February 22, 1893, when the Philadelphia & Reading Railroad failed. The Great Northern went next, then the Union Pacific, the Topeka & Santa Fe. The railroads toppled like dominoes; and their banks, having overextended themselves with unsubstantiated loans, closed their doors. People panicked. They rushed to withdraw what was left of their money in banks still standing. The runs brought on more ruination. Five hundred railroads and 15,000 companies in the United States filed bankruptcy. Unemployment ran as high as 25%. A similar panic in the United Kingdom, coupled with a drop in European trade, caused foreign investors to sell American stocks in order to obtain American funds backed by gold—driving the now global depression into dire straights in a series of knock-out punches that left men, women, and children dying in the gutters.

"Cannot the good God do something to relieve his wretched children?" Ignatius Donnelly wrote, "Or is this thing to go on forever?"

It went on. And got worse.

December 21, 1896, after having withstood the previous Panic, the National Bank of Illinois failed. It had invested $2.4 million in

continued on p. 19

છ

July 29, 1897, was not the first time Captain and Ben Moore heard of the gold. When the *Queen* flooded their beach with the first wave of Klondikers, news of the Yukon gold was for them old news. Let's back up.

To begin, "Mooresville" was never Captain Moore's property. The 160-acre homestead had been filed under Ben's name as a trading and manufacturing site. Father and son, though, did regard the claim as theirs, an equal partnership. Perhaps the land had been filed under Ben's name because Captain Moore was mired in bankruptcy. The courts simply couldn't seize what wasn't his.

Neither of them lived there. They fed the project by working in various sawmills and canneries and transporting freight on the Inside Passage—making forays whenever possible to "prove up." Early in 1895, Ben headed up for a more permanent go.

At the time, Mooresville was little more than a rustic bunkhouse, a meager wharf, a few attempts at clearing the trail, and the original cabin—without flooring, doors, a proper roof, or window coverings. But aboard the *Rustler* that day, Ben met seven California prospectors headed for the Interior. He talked them into trying the untried White Pass.

He lightered ashore their five tons of equipment, borrowed two horses from John Healy, then set out to guide the prospectors up the untried trail, hauling their equipment over the pass—proving it could be done.

The following year, Spring 1896, the captain and Ben went into partnership with a British investment company—exchanging half interest in their homestead for a cash advance of $1800. Simultaneously, the captain wangled a

CAPTAIN WILLIAM MOORE 1896 MAIL DELIVERY
by the Author/from a photograph

Canadian government contract to deliver the Royal Mail between Victoria and the Yukon: to be paid $600 for each of three separate (but overlapping) routes. Knowing he could count on Ben to help with the overlap, he arrived in Mooresville mid-May 1886, where it was agreed between them that Ben would take the middle, shorter contract (Juneau to Juneau), leaving the captain to take the first and third, and longer, deliveries (Victoria to Victoria). The old man left Mooresville May 26, 1896, with 104 pounds of mail, provisions for the entire trip, and enough lumber to build a boat on the other side of the mountains.

Acting with their newly formed British alliance (the Alaska and Northwest Territory Trading Company—A&NWTT Co.), Ben headed for Juneau to purchase supplies and hire workers to build a floating dock, a sawmill, another bunkhouse, outbuildings, and continue the trailwork. Interestingly, both father and son were delivering the mail when Skookum Jim discovered the gold that August. Captain Moore had just gotten into Victoria and Ben was in the Yukon, just a few days past discovery country—the Klondike River mouth.

Within a month Ben was back in Juneau. Compelled now by a sense of urgency, Ben hired more men. It would take a year before news of Jim's gold strike could reach the Outside. All that fall, through the winter, and into the next summer the A&NWTT Co. put up an additional $50,000 and sent up several more workers from Victoria. A frenzied time. *But where was his father*? wondered Ben. The first mail run had taken the old man four months. Six months had now passed. *Had some tragedy overtaken him*?

Record cold and early ice on the rivers had, in fact, forced Captain Moore to dogsled out of the Yukon instead of taking a steamship, thus delaying his return to Victoria until late February 1897. He'd actually gotten stuck in the hastily built Klondike town where the discovery had been made. After mushing hundreds of miles in adverse conditions his dogs had played out. But Dawson City, center of the gold rush, in December of 1896 was not a bad place to be stuck.

Prospectors already in the Yukon had bee-lined for this former moose swamp, a land bench tucked into the elbow of the Klondike and Yukon Rivers—and the growing tent city had become a beehive of stampeders swarming the surrounding creeks for gold. The delay actually allowed the captain to send someone back up to Forty Mile (government seat) to file a claim on his own behalf—and to give his friend William Ogilvie, Canada's Dominion Surveyor, opportunity to write Ottawa with an updated report on the gold—as much as $500 a day coming out of Rabbit Creek (renamed Bonanza) and the little tributary flowing into it, Eldorado. Unfortunately for Captain Moore, the small print in the mining rules required that claims be filed in person—his was jumped. But Moore's Eldorado had never been the gold. It had always been Mooresville and he chaffed at the delays.

Finally! Dogs healed and on his way again, the mail contracts at last fulfilled, and having written his final report in Victoria on March 1, 1897, he headed once more for Mooresville, leaving behind the ever forbearing Hendrika, as well as their youngest daughter Gertrude. They'd not move up for another year. In the meantime, he and Ben and the A&NWTT Co. worked to get Mooresville and the trail ready for the masses to come.

July 14, 1897, they declared White Pass open; they thought they were ready.

July 29, 1897, the stampeders arrived.

They were so not ready.

Skagway: It's All About The Gold

yet another unprofitable railroad. The massive collapse of the National Bank of Illinois—the largest failure to this point—created yet another knock-out round that saw bankers jumping from windows. The Panic of 1896 was on.

The poorest starved in the bitter winter months. Many abandoned their families, tramped the countryside, appeared at strangers' doors pleading for work, for food, a night's sleep in a haystack. Those who managed to hang onto their jobs were less effected by the crisis but felt the pinch nonetheless—and began blaming the unemployed for the increasing sorry state of affairs. The depression held on like a rabid dog, and the employed accused the unemployed of laziness, of further dragging down the economy. Stories of despair and suicide ran almost daily in newspapers and over the air waves. *For those sitting most comfortably? Buffered from the harsh reality around them?* They began to fear anarchy as tension mounted. Anger simmered, bubbled, boiled over. When a series of labor conflicts broke out, the cocooned condemned the strikers for the violence while others sadly shook their heads: They understood the untenable plight of the unemployed and underpaid.

Which is why, when the *Excelsior* put into San Francisco mid-July 1897, bearing hundreds of thousands of dollars in gold, hope ignited. Gold! Treasure lying on the ground! Waiting to be picked up! To be shovelled, wrote historian Pierre Berton, "into club bags."

A kind of lunacy, Berton wrote, "seized the continent" and on the morning of July 19, 1897, three days after the *Excelsior* had put into

Word come about the big gold strike up on the Yukon. I figgered if gold was laying around on the ground up there I might as well give in to myself, and start getting my outfit together.

—Montgomery Hawthorne

San Francisco, 5,000 people jammed Seattle's Schwabacher's Dock to greet the *Portland*—and the sixty-eight "Klondikers" reported to have been paupers made rich in some far away place called the Klondike.

"Show us the gold!" the mob chanted. "Show us the gold!"

"We got millions!" hollered Frank Phiscator, holding up his poke.

The city had gone berserk. Eagerly the crowd gave way to the exiting Klondikers—hope incarnate! Symbols of relief! Bright shiny light dispelling the terrible darkness of the decade!

A ragamuffin crew, to be sure, to shine such light. Most hadn't seen civilization for years. They were rough, they were scruffy. The women amongst them were out of fashion. Still, they were the rock stars of the Gold Rush.

Clarence Berry, a fruit farmer broken by the Panic of 1893, came out with $140,000. One fellow had to hire a couple of men to help him drag a blanket off the pier—tied around $100,000. Professor Lippey, former Seattle YMCA Secretary, and his wife, staggered ashore with $85,000. William Stanley (a Seattle blacksmith) had left his son in the Yukon Klondike to continue mining; leaving him to carry home to the Missus $115,000. The Missus—having been left to her own devices in Seattle—was bent over a laundry bucket scrubbing a client's linens when she got word. She dropped her scrub brush, kicked the bucket, and went on a shopping spree. "The latest in Paris fashions. Please," she said, heading for the nearest dressmaker's.

William Sloat, $52,000.

Henry Anderson hauled ashore $45,000.

Frank Keller, $35,000.

Con Statmatin returned with $33,000—his third interest in a claim that gave up $99,000 in 45 days.

Robert Kooks brought back $14,000 in gold dust and $12,000 from the sale of his claim.

Jack Horner from Tacoma was called unlucky. He had only $6,000. But in 1897 this was no small fortune.

GOLD! GOLD! GOLD! GOLD! Seattle's newspapers headlined. Telegraph lines tap-tapped it around the world. GOLD! GOLD IN THE KLONDIKE! Overnight, a burdened world breathed in hope like a drowning man air and no one hiccuped when J. Hobart, associate

Skagway: It's All About The Gold

editor of the *Engineering and Mining Journal,* poo-pooed the news, stating that "only the hardiest and most experienced miners could hope to prosper in that desolate land." He was right, but when you're drowning, who cares if the buoy just tossed you is full of holes?

Millions the world over schemed and dreamed of getting to Canada's frozen North. Berton writes that within twenty-four hours 2,000 people in New York bought tickets for the Klondike.

THE SEATTLE POST-INTELLIGENCER

VOL. XXXIL. No. 62   Saturday, July 19, 1897

GOLD! GOLD! GOLD! GOLD!

Sixty-Eight Rich Men on the Steamer Portland.

STACKS OF YELLOW METAL!

Some Have $5,000, Many Have More, and a Few Bring Out $100,000 Each.

THE STEAMER CARRIES $700,000.

Special Tug Chartered by the Post-Intelligencer to Get the News.

Within a week, hundreds quit their jobs; within a month, thousands. He describes the exodus: "Streetcar operators deserted their trams, policemen their beats, clergymen their congregations. Clerks walked out of offices, salesmen jumped counters, reporters quit their desks." William Haskell of Massachusetts wrote of himself:

> ...at twenty-two I was behind a counter in a big dry-good store in Boston. It took very little time for me to discover that there was no romance in the life of a dry-goods clerk... All my inclinations were to drift about, to find adventure, to see life in its various phases, and there I was day after day for long hours in a crowded corner... Variety, there was none...

> I knew I was not in my right place...stuck up in a corner like a house plant.

He, too, turned in his notice. The mania was on.

Lillian Oliver saw a way to save her husband's life. Friends were going to the Klondike and she got no sleep until she'd determined to go with them. "I fancied I saw how I could save a precious life. I dreamed of rich finds; and bags of gold haunted me all day and at night troubled my rest. I saw in my mind's eye the vision of a proud wife bearing home to a long-suffering man the wherewithal to take him away from dreary toil." She imagined a return of color to his cheeks "so long missing," and "fire come to the eye grown dim; elasticity to steps grown weak; and happiness to both of us."

Everywhere a fellow went, talk of the Klondike prevailed. William Haskell wrote: "Wherever I went, I heard little but 'Klondike' talked about on the cars, in the hotels in the saloons, and even on Sundays at church. Whenever you observed a knot of men in the street, in a rural highway, or in any public place...you were pretty sure to find that the latest news of new strike in the Klondike diggings was under discussion."

Ezra Meeker of Puyallup, WA, his hops farm and fortune wiped out the year before, decided that if farming had quit him, he'd invest in the Gold Rush.

And so, worldwide, a million people schemed and dreamed. One hundred thousand actually started out—among them William Haskell, Lillian Oliver, and Ezra Meeker.

Cities like San Francisco, Seattle, Vancouver, and Victoria swelled, then burst at the seams as these stampeders arrived, jamming their streets, choking the roadways, stuffing hotels, crowding restaurants, buying grubstakes as fast as store clerks could restock. Down on the waterfronts, boats rotting in dry dock were pressed into service. Condemned ships in the boneyards were resurrected. Sea captains sold tickets faster than hotcakes, charging ten times the rate, doubling, tripling (in some cases worse!) the legal capacity without regard to safety. A passenger wrote that his ship was "a floating bedlam, pandemonium let loose, the black hole of Caluctta in an Arctic setting." Such ships capsized, they went up on the rocks. One captain, ignoring the laws that prohibited transporting passengers and dynamite together, blew up *enoute* to Skagway. Sixty-five people died. A dog survived. Still, abandoned relics were salvaged to take the lost ships' places. And men, frantic to board, bribed the more reluctant captains, and men on the streets waylaid those with tickets. Hope, ignited, burst into flame, burning hearts with a searing heat in an unrelenting, irrational drive to get to the Klondike, to get there first, to get that gold, to get their share before it was too late.

For those who didn't go, gold begot gold. Everywhere, people peddled their wares in the name of the Klondike. Anything with the word "KLONDIKE" in it sold: KLONDIKE flour, KLONDIKE

continued on p. 25

22

— "I GOT TO HAVE FIRST-RATE STUFF" —
by Montgomery Hawthorne

CR

I told Mama we'd need to be getting my outfit together....so right after the first of the year we went up to Portland, so's I could get my outfit. You never seen nothing like it. Everyone on the street was talking about going to Alaska. They was jammed in at the grocery stores getting their grub, and packing it any which way. Mostly they was buying beans. They'd put in a few other items, and then they'd say, "Guess, you better give me a few more beans." Everything was high, beans brought 25 cents a pound. I had a pretty good idea of what I wanted and how I wanted it put up. But I didn't know where to go to find first-rate grub...

So, I hunted around until I found Dresser's store. Then I waited until I could see him personal. I looked him in the eye, and I says, "Mr. Dresser, I got to have a year's supply of grub. It's got to be first-rate stuff. This list can be changed at your suggestion, but I've given it considerable thought. I want baking powder, soda, flour, sugar, chocolate in tin cans, bacon, shortening, syrup, rice, beans, canned milk, dried pears, peaches, apples, raisins, and prunes. You can follow down the list. I want fifty pounds of dates. I tell you, man, this outfit has got to last me for at least a year..."

I told Mr. Dresser I wanted my stuff packed in heavy canvas bags, without any stamping on them and he agreed to supply them. I wanted each bag to have a number on it. Then I had him write what was in each bag in a little book. I knowed I'd have to leave my stuff along the trail and I wanted to make it confusing for anyone up there who tried to rob my cache. Anybody up there doing any stealing would be doing it because he'd run out of something. If he picked up one of my sacks, he'd have no way of telling what he was getting.

After we had ordered my grub, Mama and me hunted around a long time to get my clothes. I couldn't pack much with me. I figgered what I took had to be made good. I got a stout mackinaw coat, two weights of shirts, red flannel underwear, two heavy pairs of wool pants,

and three big pairs of cotton pants. You see, the cotton overalls had to be big enough to go on over top of the wool ones. You could freeze to death in wool. The wind goes right through it. But if you got cotton on the outside of wool, you keep all the heat of your body in and have the warm wool right against you. Then when it warms up you can shed them heavy pants...

Then I went down to Honeyman's to get my miner's supplies. A lot of other fellows was getting outfitted there, too. Most of them didn't know nothing about the North, or mining, or boat building. There was a lot of talk, but not much real planning going on. As soon as I could get a clerk, I started reading my list, and picking each item careful. I loaded up heavy on ammunition for my high powered rifle, a 30-40 Winchester, and for my .44 six shooter Colt's revolver. After that I ordered a cast iron, fold-up stove with a kind of a Dutch oven. I got my pans, and a skillet, and a couple of strong water buckets. I knowed better than to buy a lantern, kerosene is hard to carry. And a big box of candles lasts a long time. A man can cut a side out of a tin can and make a reflector and wind break both for his candlelight.

Why, I even had to get a new tent. And two hickory sleds. They was regular Yukon sleds, and made light and strong. They cost seven dollars apiece. But they had been made for the trail, being about twelve inches off the ground, and sixteen inches wide and six foot long... By that time we was wore out. I'd rather pack all day over a trail than go shopping. I got Mama a new dress, then we went back to Astoria on the boat. The groceries was to come down later, and be held on the dock...until I was ready to sail, but the rest of the outfit needed considerable working over. Seemed like I was getting a terrible big outfit, but I had learned to figger ahead... I'd rather spend my time figgering here than worrying there.

...Mama had my bedding fixed; and she knit me several pairs of mittens and a pile of the finest wool socks I ever did see, and two wool caps. She made a little bag for my sewing kit. Then she boiled a bunch of old linen napkins, and fixed them for bandages. She put in some medicines, too. A man hasn't no business going on a long trip without Epsom's salt, and tincture of benzoine, and turpentine, at least. She hemmed up some pieces of mosquito netting to go over my wide brimmed hat, with a draw string to pull in around my neck. And she put in some bars of real good homemade soap...

I was all ready. My outfit was packed in tight canvas bags and was down at the docks. My name was put in for a ticket.

boots, KLONDIKE tents, bags, and stoves. Berton wrote that the word "Klondike" was attached "on coffee lozenges, evaporated eggs, dried onions, beef blocks, peanut meals." The word "Klondike" was pasted to gold pans, beds, boats, scurvy cures, "even X-ray machines," he wrote, "designed to detect the presence of golden treasure."

The *world* had gone berserk.

Anarchy

Such were the hordes who splashed ashore in Mooresville/ Skagway on July 29, 1897, pitching their tents, building hotels, and thumbing their noses at the legalities of property rights. The lure of gold and money to be made had skewed the moral compass of decent men.

It beckoned, too, all the riffraff known to frontier America: prostitutes, gamblers, thieves, thugs, artful con men. King of these bottom dwellers was Jefferson Randolph Smith, and he arrived in Skagway on the 22nd of August with a trio of thugs one step ahead of Colorado law and just three weeks behind the first rush of miners. Slick, smart, seductive, "Soapy" Smith was a seasoned swindler and manipulative crime lord who once controlled "every piece of grift in Denver and Creede and took a rake-off from every saloon and hose in both cities." Nicknamed for the soap con he'd perfected—selling small bars of soap for five bucks a piece by tricking greedy crowds into thinking they had a fair shot at getting one wrapped in a twenty, fifty, or even a hundred dollar bill—his slight of hand kept the money rolling in. The least of his sins. He got away with this and worse because he knew how to play "every cop and politician who could be bought—and a few who couldn't." But like Captain Moore (and Dave McKinney and

ALL THINGS KLONDIKE
Ypsilantian, Oct 6, 1898
Ypsilanti, Michigan

THE SEATTLE POST-INTELLIGENCER
VOL. XXXII. No. 62   Saturday, July 19, 1897

GOLD! GOLD! GOLD! GOLD!

Sixty-Eight Rich Men on the Steamer Portland.

STACKS OF YELLOW METAL!

Some Have $5,000, Many Have More, and a Few Bring Out $100,000 Each.

THE STEAMER CARRIES $700,000.

Special Tug Chartered by the Post-Intelligencer to Get the News.

Frank Reid), Soapy understood the mother lode not to be the Klondike River in the Yukon but the "Klondikers" passing through Skagway.

Forget the tedious task of building a sawmill or standing long hours behind a bar, serving men rotgut for an hourly wage. Soapy's idea of Eldorado was to plumb the Klondikers crazy for gold, men in a hurry, men with no time to stop and press charges. The locals could be had by tossing a few dollars at their charities: a few to the church and a widow of two. Such was the knit and purl of Soapy's law-and-order persona, a cloak designed to veil his darker deeds and ultimate goal: Absolute control of Skagway. "I am going to be the boss of Skagway," he wrote former Denver cop Willis Loomis. "I know exactly how to do it, and if you come along I'll make you chief of police."

Born in anarchy, Skagway swiftly descended into violence with Soapy's help. An early Klondiker recorded Skagway as a city of "saloons, a crap game, a faro layout...some 300 tents, and a population of about 2,000 men and seventeen women." In this clime, and in just nineteen days, Soapy and his card sharks managed to make $18,000 to $20,000. His great-grandson, Jefferson Randolph Smith II, writes that in today's currency this amounts to over half a million dollars. They split their take and headed south for reinforcements. It can be argued as to when the man came back. The point is, he came back—with a gang, and he went into silent partnership with two of the six Clancy brothers—a clan of their own who owned professional gambling halls up and down the West Coast.

Some say Soapy hooked up with Frank Reid as well, at the Klondike Saloon. That too can be argued. He did have three or four shanties of his own, where he conducted "legitimate" enterprises as fronts for his gang to fleece grubstakes off incoming Klondikers—using marked cards, armed robbery, whatever it took. His gambling halls, his non existent freight companies, his phony information bureaus were legendary, as was his "army enlistment" shed during the Spanish-American War where victims lost their clothes and possessions while undergoing a physical—although this particular shenanigan is vehemently denied by Smith II. Does it matter? Soapy's operation was effective, his machinations the steam behind an engine of audacious outlaws

Skagway: It's All About The Gold

who posed as clergymen, reporters, freighters, and knowledgeable old timers.

This is how it worked. These artful con men swarmed the docks whenever a ship put in and created a narrow trail through which the stampeding miners had to elbow their way. The "wolves" feigned eagerness to hear of outside news and in this way engaged the un-suspecting "sheep" in conversation. By carrying their luggage, they obligated their prey to drinks at a "reputable" pub. Flies to a web, these newcomers (*cheechakos*) were completely unaware they'd been singled out to be "fleeced." And if a man did cotton on and refused to be drawn in, two "tipsy" prospectors at the bar would start a fight and the poor fellow would find himself slugged in the melee and, of course, mugged.

Another ploy was to approach the more prosperous-looking men coming off the gangplanks. Slim Jim Foster liked to sidle up to them, limping, coughing a little, fairly begging the man to buy his whole kit-and-caboodle for a $100. This included two lots, he'd press, and a comfortable cabin. He had to let it go cheap, you know, because the climate was killing him. Hooked by such a good deal, the dupe would no sooner step into the cabin than another gangster packing a gun would step out of the shadows. The astonished mark would find himself locked up in a cabin not for sale while Slim Jim and his accomplice headed for one of Soapy's enterprises where they'd hand over one-sixth of the take to Soapy and split the rest between them.

A more benign con was Soapy's $5 telegram. Catering to miners anxious to report their status to folks back home, his telegraph office was a place where men eagerly passed over their coinage; eagerly again when the reply arrived; and just as eagerly, again, to meet whatever emergency the creative clerk might tell—without once bothering to look behind the shack where the cable petered out.

By mid-October Skagway's population had soared to anywhere from 10,000 to 20,000, depending on who you talked to, the Mounties reporting the initial concourse of tents growing "into a fair-sized city with well-laid out streets and numerous frame buildings." Elaborate false storefronts had gone up as well, deceptively high and with curlicues and bold colors, transforming one-story structures into two, designed to trick miners into thinking the enterprises bigger and more prosperous than they really were. The inaugural *Skagway News* debuting in the middle of the month listed them as 15 general stores, 19 restaurants, 4 meat markets, 3 wharves, 11 saloons, 6 lumber yards, 8 packing outfits, 6 lawyers, and 9 hotels. No mention was made of the brothels—dozens of them.

I'd seen Soapy around town. He was kind of a nice mannered, clean-looking fellow. He never went around talking and bragging and shoving folks. He moved quiet and soft like, but he was always figgering out how things was best for Soapy.

—Montgomery Hawthorne

Skagway: It's All About The Gold

Avarice was limited only by talent and imagination, reported Canadian Mountie Sam Steele on his way to enforce law and order at the passes. Gunfire peppered Broadway day and night. Bullets whistled through his walls and narrowly missed his head. He later wrote that Skagway was little better than hell on earth, about the roughest place in the world. His report read:

'Soapy' Smith, a 'bad man,' and his gang of about 150 ruffians ran the town and did what they pleased; almost the only persons safe from them were the members of our force. Robbery and murder were daily occurrences; many people came through with money, and next morning had not enough to get a meal, having been robbed or cheated out of their last cent. Shots were exchanged in the streets in broad daylight, and enraged Klondikers pursued the scoundrels of Soapy Smith's gang to get even with them. At night the crash of bands, shouts of 'Murder!' and cries for help mixed with the cracked voices of singers in the variety halls.

JEFFERSON RANDOLPH SMITH
by the Author/from a photograph

Dawson's *Klondike Nugget* reported Skagway as being the "boiling pot of hell where were assembled the dregs of the earth." Alexander MacDonald wrote that while he'd stumbled upon a few tough corners in the world, the most lawless quarter he ever struck was Skagway. "It seemed as if the scum of the earth," he wrote, "had hastened here to fleece and rob, or...to murder." Soapy and his boys, it seems, were villains in a town without heroes.

Heroes
There *were* heroes, though.

Brenda Wilbee

UNION CHURCH, 1897
by the Author/from a photograph

Reverend Dickey and Mollie Walsh, traveling separately but finding each other aboard ship, arrived October 9, 1897. The Presbyterian preacher, in town only for six months, wasted no time. He tacked up notices around town and preached his first sermon the next morning at Burkhard House on the southwest corner of Broadway and Fourth to a standing-room-only crowd.

Molly joined the effort by helping create the ladies' "Muffin and Crumpet" Society, and with their bake sales (and men passing the hat) enough money was raised to erect a clapboard building on Fifth Avenue, between State and Main—with an attached shanty out back for Dickey's temporary living quarters: He was just passing through *en route* to Dawson City. Even so, he had a profound influence during the brief six months he stayed in Skagway.

His Union Church went up in time for a December 12th dedication. He invited an Episcopalian bishop from Haines, AK, to come over and preach; and when he heard that a Catholic priest was in town, he invited him to participate as well. He created a Board of Trustees from the seven denominations represented in town. Within the church, he started Skagway's first YMCA reading room. The first school met here. Here the first homeless shelter was as well, destitute

Skagway: It's All About The Gold

men sleeping on the floor. "Dead brokes" they were called, and there were many.

Before Dickey left the following spring, he became a familiar figure. Through the worst of the winter, he ministered to men taken ill and dying from an outbreak of spinal meningitis. The highly contagious disease claimed lives both on the trail and in town. A man, a child, might complain in the evening of pain at the back of his or her head, grow delirious during the night, die before morning. The ill were gathered in shacks and cabins, and the best help Dicky could procure lent what little comfort could be had. His journal reveals almost daily entries of one or more deaths, and the Gold Rush Cemetery bears silent witness. Scores died. The suffering, however, prompted Reverend Dicky to build the city's first hospital.

He did not do this alone. He had Molly.

Molly Walsh was Queen of White Pass Trail and she remains Skagway's most beloved heroine. Molly grew up in an Irish neighborhood of St. Paul, MN, but life as a stenographer in a stuffy office was not an adventurous sixteen-year-old girl's bliss. She ran off in 1890 with a girlfriend to Butte, Montana.

Rumor suggests she earned her living as a dance hall girl. No one knows for sure. We do know she followed adventure. In 1893 she headed for Chicago to work at the World's Fair; and in 1897 she headed for Skagway, a gold rush town much wilder than Butte. Twenty-four, pretty, petite, a light dusting of freckles on her nose and curly red hair tied modestly behind her neck, the Irish lass defied all social norms and much-expected standards. Nonetheless, she won the affection of all— beginning the moment she stepped off the ship with Reverend Dickey.

Leaving the dance hall scene to women with names like Sweet Marie, Sitting Maude, Ethel the Moose, and Babe Wallace the Virgin, Molly worked in one of Skagway's nineteen restaurants. She worked, too, alongside the minister at his church and then nursed in his hospital. One night, risking her reputation, she went into Clancy's brothel to tend a dying childhood friend. The fatally ill prostitute asked for a priest. There being none, Molly sent for Reverend Dickey.

Never one to kowtow to convention himself, Dickey scandalously held the funeral. Close to fifty "soiled doves" (as well as the curious)

31

Brenda Wilbee

MOLLY WALSH
by the Author/from a photograph

crowded into Union Church. Today, Skagway tends to have fun with her history of prostitution; in reality, white slavery was a problem—by some reports involving girls as young as eleven. Dickey was not blind. He asked the crowd of "unfortunates" if any had the courage to begin anew. Captain Jack of the *Shamrock* offered free passage to Vancouver or Seattle. Someone put up $1,000 in way of traveling expenses. Dickey and Mollie then went to the brothels to remove the girls' meager belongings. That night thirty escaped.

The loss of revenue did not set well with the madams and men like Soapy Smith—whose organized crime dealt in the back streets of French, Paradise, and the very politically incorrect "Jap" Alleys. Targeted, Dickey weathered the attacks better than Molly. She escaped in March up the trail to Log Cabin, where the Mounties, stationed with Maxim guns and uncompromising law, insured her safety from Soapy's menacing thugs.

She pitched a tent and opened a cookhouse, serving nourishing meals to exhausted, fevered, and hungry men. She took in the penniless, tended the sick—and anyone needing a kind smile sought her out. In a stampede that produced women like Molly Fewclothes, Mollie Walsh stood the exception. Packer Jack Newman wrote that although "she fed and lodged the wildest and most persistent men Alaska ever saw, she remained as clean and morally pure as the snow that fell on her tent."

Mollie favored Jack. He'd stumbled into her tent with a frozen hand and in her touch, he said, "a strange feeling passed between us."

Others claimed a special feeling, too—including a faro dealer named Mike Bartlett. He had nothing but contempt for mule drivers, he said, Jack Newman in particular. Taunts passed up the trail.

32

Skagway: It's All About The Gold

"Something's got to be done about that braggart," Jack resolved, and in true wild-west fashion they faced each other in the street. "I won't kill him, just keep him from running up to Log Cabin," Jack declared. Minutes later, he carried the bleeding faro man to Dickey's hospital and went back to courting Mollie. Fearing that no good could come of Mike's involvement in her life, he forbade Molly to see the man.

Mollie was unaccustomed to having anyone tell her what to do.

"She said I wasn't her master," Jack later divulged. "One thing led to another. Trifle piled on trifle. Neither of us would weaken. Then Mollie up and married the skunk."

Mike, it turned out, was a not-so-nice drunk. A year and a half later, Molly fled, Mike in pursuit. He caught up with her in Seattle. He begged reconciliation. She declined. He threatened to kill himself. She caved. A few days later, on the moonless night of October 27, 1902, she ran in terror outside, clad only in a nightgown. Moments later, the Queen of White Pass Trail and friend of the destitute was dead. Shot in the back.

MOLLY WALSH
Author photograph

In 1930, Jack commissioned a bust of her likeness. "Her spirit fingers still reach across the years," he wrote, "and play on the slackened strings of my old heart, and my heart still sings—MOLLIE!—my heart still sings but in such sad undertone that none but God and I can hear."

The statue is on Sixth, east of Broadway, in downtown Skagway.

Violence

Despite the reverend and Mollie's heroic influence, Soapy Smith's villainous presence was stronger. The U.S. Commissioner, the U.S. Marshal, the newspaper editor, these were just three of the men known to be in Soapy's pay. He had other undercover spies infiltrating the community like spiders, scuttling out of the shadows in search of prey. "You never know who was who," a citizen explained. "Your next door neighbor—or the man at the next table in a restaurant—might be in his pay." The city assessor wrote that "while 'Soapy' Smith was not implicated in all the black deeds…he never failed to take the side of the guilty party, and often fought hard to have him go unpunished, no doubt anticipating that the rescued villain would not fail to do anything for him when called upon."

Illustrative of the assessor's assessment was a double murder the end of January. Bartender John Fay had killed Andy McGrath (a belligerent drunk) and Deputy Rowan (investigating the complaint). An outraged town gathered and was scouring the alleyways in high

WINTER 1898
Alaska State Library: P. E. Larrs Collection, P41-222

dungeon. Fueling their rage was the fact that Deputy Rowan's wife had just given birth to their first child. Soapy, just three days back from the Lower 48 with fresh recruits, threatened wholesale slaughter if anyone so much as harmed a hair of bartender Fay's head.

A possible lynching short-stopped, Soapy then went to work behind the scenes, manipulating events his way. When the thwarted town met in Union Church to see if justice could yet be served, Soapy sent spies to direct the decisions while he himself made the more public display of soliciting funds for the widow and her newborn infant—his own name and generous donation topping the subscription list.

Reverend Dickey summarized the whole messy affair in a letter to his wife:

> A lynching bee in the church! And the Robin Hood of the town controlling that meeting and practically nominating the committees; and the desperado at the same time protecting the murderer and taking up a public subscription for the relief of the widow of his victim.

A masterful con. With one stroke, Soapy had painted himself hero of law and order, friend to the destitute, and generous benefactor. That same week, the *Seattle-Post Intelligencer* reported Skagway's lawlessness as being beyond description, Soapy in complete control, citizens afraid to speak out, holdups, robberies, shootings routine. Soapy himself wrote a Seattle friend the end of February: "We have got them licked and mean to rule absolutely."

By March, Soapy must have felt secure enough to openly run his den of iniquity, for on the 9th he ran an ad, announcing the opening of his oyster bar at JEFF. SMITHS PARLOR. Always a hot bed for gambling and dance hall girls, 317 Sixth Avenue quickly became known as the "real city hall" and Soapy ascended to the dizzy heights of uncrowned King of Skagway.

Crime stood at an all-time high. Two days prior to putting up his shingle, Alexander McLain had been robbed right outside his home. The next day twelve robberies occurred on the trail. Near Porcupine Hill, Peter Bean was found with a .38 caliber slug to his chest. A week later Sam Roberts was killed and down on the beach a nameless man was robbed, knocked unconscious, and tossed off a wharf. Investigations were cursory, without finding. Naturally. Deputy Marshall Taylor was in Soapy's pay.

At first, Skagway's businessmen had been willing to look the other way in exchange for being left unmolested. They now realized that Soapy's shadow had lengthened and darkened; and Frank Reid, Skagway's self-appointed surveyor, became the lightning rod around which the opposition rallied. The Committee of 101, formed in October to file the lawsuit against Ben Moore over property rights, reconvened; and JEFF. SMITHS PARLOR hadn't been open a week when the town woke to notices posted by the Committee, threatening action if "objectionable characters" didn't leave town.

Soapy's hackles shot up. He countered with a public rally, and with cool gray eyes and seductive oratory, he pronounced the Committee of 101 as newcomers, vigilantes, acting outside the law—and he nailed up his own posters:

> The body of men styling themselves the Committee of 101 are hereby notified that any overt act committed by them will promptly be met with

continued on p. 39

JEFF. SMITHS PARLOR, EXTERIOR
by the Author/from a photograph

— A KID'S PERSPECTIVE —
by Royal Pullen

❦

Royal Pullen was a kid in 1897, ten years old. Soapy was a kind of hero to him. He described JEFF. SMITHS PARLOR in an interview just before his 100th birthday.

"It didn't have anything very plush. There were red curtains in the saloon, but not in the restaurant. There were just tables with oils cloth on them… He had a little restaurant in there, and then the gambling hall and saloon was right next to it, and that's where he entertained us newsboys.

"He had little tables… I guess there must have been 25 or 30 of us news kids, and an oyster dinner was really something. He had a back room that was his office, where they carried on. I was never allowed back in there… We were 10- and 11-year-old kids. They don't allow you around. They'd say, 'Sonny, go on, this is no place for you.'

"He was a good guy as far as we were concerned. He liked us kids, and we liked Soapy. He wasn't mean. There wasn't anything about Soapy that was mean. He always would pay us. The boy who got to him first with the news from the states got a silver dollar because it took the papers anywhere from a week to two weeks to get there. Those old gamblers and panhandlers were really nice. I had a lot of friends amongst them, I really did."

JEFF. SMITH'S PARLOR, INTERIOR
by the Author/from a photograph

—— Skagway In The Days Of Soapy ——
by Clara Dedman of the Pacific and Golden North Hotels

CR

I t was on the anniversary of my birth, July 5th, 1898, that I arrived in Skagway. As the ship...approached the wharf there were only a few stragglers and half a dozen dogs in sight, but as soon as the steamer whistle blew, people and dogs began to appear from every direction, and by the time we docked there were several hundred beings and at least 300 dogs of every imaginable breed waiting to welcome us.

My husband met me at the wharf and put me and my belongings into an ancient express wagon. As we jogged along Main Street I expected every minute that I would be thrown out, or the wagon would overturn, for the road was full of large mud holes and tree stumps, anywhere from two to five feet high... We reached my new house on Eleventh Street safely, however...At the time of my arrival the whole town was seething with unrest, primarily owing to the activities of Soapy Smith and his gang, who were at the height of their power, and were accused of jumping lots and committing] many robberies and much violence. Personally, I don't think Soapy was ever quite as bad as people made him out to be, but on the other hand, he wasn't by any means a good influence in the community...

When I reached Skagway the population was about 10,000 men, 350 dance-hall women, 11 legitimate wives, two dozen children from seven years old up, and two or three young babies. The ship I went in on brought nine more wives, and additional ones arrived on every subsequent steamer. My son, who was born shortly after my arrival, was the first child to be born of white parents in Skagway.

In [the Pacific Hotel] my husband and I installed the first bath tub in Skagway. It was in use day and night and the first month

cleared us $150. For four, or five, months we had a monopoly of the bathing business in the town and then a local barber put in three tubs and others followed suit. It was quite evident from the rushing business all the baths did that men would keep clean if only they had the opportunity.

...in 19[08]...we left the Pacific. The Golden North has been my home ever since and I have conducted it since the death of Mr. Dedman in 1925.

Skagway: It's All About The Gold

the law abiding citizens of Skagway and...the Law and Order Society, consisting of 317 citizens will see that justice is dealt out to it fullest extent...

Skagway was confused. *Who stood for law and? The so-called vigilantes? Or Soapy Smith?* "Jeff Smith, he's a good fellow," his network of spies said, handing out lies like marked cards at a fixed game. "He's generous. He's public-spirited."

And of course he was, launching the Adopt-A-Dog program, taking in six dogs from the hundreds in the streets and sending the rest to Seattle—where he promised to have them adopted out. No one knew, of course, that once in Seattle his men sold the dogs for $250 a piece to miners buying tickets on any old tub that would take them north, circulating the dogs right back to Skagway. But, hey, sure, Soapy's a good guy, and by the end of April he was again the uncrowned king of Skagway—leaving Frank Reid's Committee of 101 to watch in silence as Soapy gained alarming ascendancy.

By July, he was untouchable. He rode in the 4th of July parade. He sat next to the governor. He commanded a militia of his own men. Three days later a miner arrived in town with $2,800 of gold. Soapy stole it.

The nuggets and gold dust represented eighteen months in the Klondike. The morning after J. D. Stewart arrived, he made the worst mistake of his life. He headed up Broadway and around the corner to Jeff Smith's Parlor.

JOHN D. STEWART
by the Author/from a photograph

"So did you *see* who robbed you?" U.S. Deputy Marshall Taylor asked when Stewart made his complaint. "*No?* So what makes you think I can help you? *I* certainly didn't see him," said the deputy, in line for his share of the take once the dust settled. "Go back to the Klondike," he added. "Get yourself another poke."

At the time, U.S. commissioners, marshals, and deputy

39

marshals were unpaid. They were expected to live off the fees and fines collected from prisoners who either pled guilty—or who'd been found guilty. Prison and death sentences were not paying situations. The overall situation was ripe for corruption, and unscrupulous men like Deputy Marshal Taylor found it more lucrative to accept bribes and look the other way. He showed J. D. Stewart the door and went home to supervise some carpentry work being done on his new house.

But unlike hundreds before him, Stewart refused to go away. He hounded the recently appointed U.S. Commissioner (replacing the corrupt John U. Smith). He hounded George DeWitt, owner of a large packing outfit. DeWitt took him down to Charlie Sperry's warehouse on the docks where packers, like himself, stored the freight they'd been hired to haul over the pass. Grocer John Kalem was there. So was Si Tanner, a well-respected hardware man. And Frank Reid. All were members of the Committee of 101.

"When word gets down river," De Witt fumed, "that the first man coming through Skagway was robbed, no one will come this way!" Frank Reid agreed. "And it'll so embolden Soapy," said Tanner, "we'll never see the end of it."

The Committee of 101 had no authority to act. Until the federal government extended the right of local rule, not even the *ad hoc* city council could enforce its edicts. Yet something had to be done. "We need the community behind us," said Frank Reid. "Let's get the town together. See if anyone has any ideas." Mr. E. O. Sylvester volunteered his Klondike Trading Company as a meeting place. They set the time for eight that evening.

In the meantime, a new U.S. Commissioner followed through on Stewart's complaint. He and a handful of 101 Committee members paid Soapy a call. Judge Shelbourne ordered him to return the poke by 4:00 or else. An empty threat known to all. Shelbourne could only act under martial law.

That night, the Klondike Trading Company was packed. Catherine Spude writes that although "Smith had wisely chosen to stay in his saloon, his cronies riddled the audience, and soon had the hall in a state of chaos, peppering...irrelevant questions and bringing up issues with no bearing on the theft." Cooler heads prevailed.

Skagway: It's All About The Gold

E. O. SYLVESTER'S KLONDIKE TRADING COMPANY, 1898
TODAY'S GOLDEN NORTH HOTEL
by the Author/from a photograph

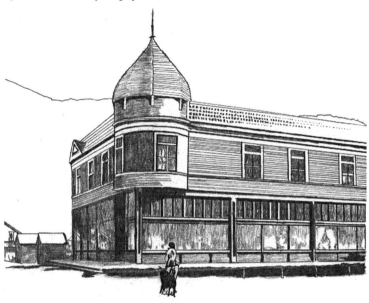

They brought the meeting to an end, to be reconvened at nine, down in Sylvester's warehouse on the end of Juneau Dock. This time, the Committee decided to post guards.

Much has been written about Soapy Smith and Frank Reid as they danced their way to the big showdown at the end of Juneau Dock that balmy summer night of July 8th, 1898. The legend is essentially this: Although it was nine o'clock at night, the Alaskan summer sunlight was still bright; strong enough for a man to read his paper without turning on a lamp. And Soapy, generally a moderate drinker, had been drinking heavily all afternoon in the "real city hall," contemplating his options with the most trusted of his men. The 4:00 deadline had come and gone. A disquietude had fallen over the town and the streets were quiet. People somberly went about their business. Dogs, sensing the tension, had holed up under the porches and were whimpering into their paws. Even his own men were beginning to tuck in their tails.

"What's that Tripp?" Soapy growled. "You got something to say?"

Old Man Tripp, one of three men who'd snatched the gold, mumbled something about maybe they ought to give the money back. Make up some kind of story —

"I'll cut the ears off the first man to make such a move," snapped Soapy. "We got this town where we want it. Give it up now? That would be selling our birthright! We're not doing that!. *I'm* not doing that! Not because some damn fool lost his poke in a card game!"

Slim Jim glanced to the trunk secreting the stolen money. Soapy stopped him with an icy stare even as a rap at the door brought in Reporter Billy Saportas. Billy had been down at the warehouse ostensibly to cover the story but secretly spying for Soapy. He held out a note. Reverend Bowers crossed the small room to take the slip of paper. Like the rest of them, he knew better than to open it. He handed it off to the boss. Soapy read it once, in silence. *The crowd is angry. If you want to do anything, do it quick.*

He lurched to his feet, a jolt of rage turning the gray of his eyes a gun metal slate. "Who the hell are these people to turn on me?" he demanded of no one in particular. "Haven't I taken care of their poor, their sick? Haven't I given money to their insufferable causes?" Liquor-revved, hopping mad, he slipped a derringer up his sleeve, dropped a revolver into a pocket. "*Ingrates!*" he roared. "High time I teach these sons-of-a-bitch bastards a lesson! I'll drive the lot of them into the bay!" He slung his .30/.30 Winchester over a shoulder and stormed outside, headed for Juneau Dock. Fourteen nervous men followed, hands ready on their guns — but keeping a safe distance.

"Go on! Go on to bed!" Soapy snarled at a knot of idlers as he rounded the corner off Sixth onto State. He reached Third and was crossing the street when he met his business partner John Clancy out for a walk with his wife and six-year-old son.

"You're asking for trouble," Clancy said, "going down there. Sit tight, Jeff. Let this blow over. I tell you, it will."

"You leave me alone, Johnny."

"They're in an ugly mood. Someone's going to get hurt."

Soapy stuck the barrel of his Winchester into Clancy's belly.

"Whoa!" Clancy wheezed, taking a snappy step back. "Go on then, go on, get yourself killed."

Skagway: It's All About The Gold

State Street ran onto Juneau Dock. Solid ground gave way to pilings as Soapy thundered onto the planking, boots thumping. Eleven-year-old Royal Pullen, standing on his back porch a few hundred feet away, said, "All this crowd, and Soapy came down, he was drunk, see?"

Two men on the dock itself, overseeing a bit of railroad equipment being unloaded, looked up.

"By the Lord," said one, "here comes Soapy! Now look out!"

For a moment the pair paused, hands on their hips. "Nonsense," summarized the other dismissively, going back to work. "He's just bluffing."

"I don't know," the first said.

Soapy shoved past three of four guards but was blocked by his nemisis, Frank Reid—who stood arms crossed, feet planted.

"Damn you!" Soapy hissed, weaving ever so slightly on his own feet from the abrupt stop. "I should have done something about you last March! You're the source of all my trouble!"

Frank Reid had faced danger before, fighting Indians. He'd killed a man, too, in an Oregon bar room brawl.

43

"Can't let you go down there, Jeff, not tonight," he said with a condescending tone that rankled Soapy to the bone.

"I have every right to hear what's being said behind my back. You can't hold a trial...without the defendant."

"The defendant was supposed to show up at four o'clock with John Stewart's poke."

Quick as lightning, Soapy struck Reid a blow to the head with the Winchester. Staggering, Reid went for his pistol.

"My God, man, don't shoot!" shouted Soapy.

Too late. Bullets flew.

Soapy dropped with a thunk to the dock. Reid collapsed in agonizing pain. Soapy, unconscious, gurgling blood, died within minutes.

San Francisco Chronicle, July 24, 1898, Public Domain.

Skagway: It's All About The Gold

It took Reid twelve days to die. Shot through the groin, pelvis shattered, his was an agonizing death.

But Skagway lived happily ever after. That's the legend.

Not so, says Soapy's great-grandson. The real hero was a guard named Murphy. Politics, Jefferson Randolph Smith II insists, wrote the fantastic fiction casting Frank Reid as the savior firing an assassin's bullet. Spude agrees. Personally, I think Skagway, conceived in speculation, birthed in anarchy, and fed by violence, needed a savior to cleanse her sins. Someone had to slay the dragon and Frank Reid made the better hero. An unlikely one, true, seeing as how he'd played a lead role in the collective theft of Ben Moore's land and he'd somehow escaped a questionable murder rap in Oregon. But he was a martyr and he was dead. A dead martyr in any mythology calls trump.

So Skagway called trump and moved on. She was Alaska's first incorporated city—and biggest. Her population held steady at 8- to 10,000, and more than a 1,000 miners were passing through each month. There was fantastic money to be made.

Competition

From the start, beginning with Johnny Healy telling Captain Moore that he'd never heard of a second pass through the mountains, Dyea and Skagway had been competing for the lucrative Klondike market—a kind of tug-of-war between the two towns. Little infrastructure existed in the Yukon, certainly no Costco, and so when the gold rush began in earnest the Canadian government issued a "ton of goods" rule to ward off starvation. Everyone going into the Canada had to take 2,000 pounds of grub and gear, enough to last them a year. For Skagway and Dyea it meant "mine the miners" and every thrown-together store had her bacon and beans for sale. Contest on, Dyea hawked her Chilkoot Trail, Skagway her White Pass, each town hiring lobbyists at $100 a day to haunt each other's beaches, to dissuade and persuade every incoming miner that her trail was best. In reality, both were the devil's own.

Getting to the gold was no seven-day stroll through the mountains as advertised by the newspapers in the Lower 48 and around the world. "Whichever way you go," a miner who'd tried them both said, "you'll wish you'd gone the other." Another said, "One's hell. The other's damnation." Journalist Tappan Adney, reporting for *Harper's Weekly* and the *London Chronicle,* debated.

He'd arrived in Skagway August the 20th. Men like Frank Reid were just settling in. Soapy would arrive in two days' time. It would be another three weeks before "widow" Harriet Pullen arrived—an enterprising woman destined to etch her name in Skagway's history. But for the hundreds of nameless men and women swarming the beach and looking to get over the mountains before winter fell, the preying question was this: *Which trail to take?*

Dreaming of wealth and having left home to get it, this was a dilemma. Every day counted, every minute—*but which trail?* Do they hike the thirty-three miles over the Chilkoot, the higher pass, or take the longer forty-four miles up the lower White Pass? More miles, yes, but horses could make it through. Yet disheartened men were retreating off White Pass to toss good money at packers standing by to take their kit-and-caboodle over to Dyea and the Chilkoot. *Which trail?*

Ever the reporter, Adney decided to take both.

White Pass Trail

The White Pass Trail was not yet a month old when he embarked. Hundreds had already gone ahead, hundreds more would follow—an unending string of unseasoned dreamers who'd left their desks and easy life to strike it rich. The first mile was easy enough and put Adney in mind of a newly cut road through the Adirondack forests; the open path, the flanking cottonwood and spruce, the hemlock, the white birch bringing light to the density, the earth packed hard and smooth. A mile and a half in he crossed the first of Captain Moore's log bridges, east to west over Skagway River, the current below running swiftly, evenly, but strong enough, he noticed, to "bear a man off his feet, even though no deeper than to his knees." Scattered tents nested the trail for another two miles, banking the river's west side. As the valley narrowed, the tents thickened and began to hatch like so many mushrooms on the forest floor. Suddenly, a clearing and a noisy riot of activity! Here was the foot of the hill. Here was the end of the valley.

Skagway: It's All About The Gold

FOOT OF THE HILL
Alaska State Library: Winter and Pond Collection, ASL-P21-10

Here a woman baked biscuits over a fire, selling them hot, twelve for a dollar. Here a prostitute sat on a stump, swinging her leg, showing some ankle and singing a merry ditty. Here two men argued over their outfit. Here everyone divided their gear into manageable loads—here they began the task of relaying 2,000 pounds of gear and grub uphill in shifts, six or seven miles at a time. Here easy was over. Here hell began.

Picture this. A mountain of boulders, all sizes, jumbled in a pile and knit together with threads of moss and loam and riddled through with trees and granite and trickling water. The sight must have stopped a man's breath, and it must have crossed Adney's mind that the Mounties just behind him (a contingent headed for the Yukon with seventy-four horses) would be in for a rough time. He left his own horse behind.

On foot, he scrabbled up the narrow path to the left, ribboning up the mountainside. Up he went, zigzagging a cliff "so covered with luxurious vegetation," he wrote, "that the heights above and the depths below did not impress." At every turn the narrow trail narrowed yet more. The banks dropped a hundred feet, two hundred, and it seemed to him, he wrote, "as if nothing could prevent a loaded horse from going clear over."

At the summit of Porcupine Hill he saw his first victim—a horse lying at the foot of the bank, twenty feet down, beside a small stream.

Brenda Wilbee

Farther on he encountered a trail jam, everyone waiting in the tight embrace of the forest. A horse had tumbled between boulders. Only its head was sticking out, but it was alive. Moving on again, he found boulders that afforded no foothold; hidden holes that twisted a man's ankle; swamps that sucked him down to his knees. He crisscrossed creeks and rivulets and sloshed up to his knees in mire, everyone ahead and behind stained brown. Wearily, they made their beds on stumps in the brush, rain drizzling off their hats, putting out their fires, dampening their enthusiasm, tearing at their souls.

A fifty-four-year-old fellow who'd been around the block a time or two confided that he'd seen worse trails for a short distance. "But this is the worst I have ever seen for the distance. I went in over the trail when it was first cut through, and I called it then a good trail, but I predict that if the rains keep up it will be impossible to get a horse over."

This was the problem unforeseen by Captain Moore and his son Ben—the slippery mess made by hundreds of men tromping over the same narrow path in the unrelenting rain. Nor could they have predicted the cruelty of men desperate to cross the mountains before winter. Horses were overloaded, worked to exhaustion, whipped unmercifully, and then abandoned when a leg, slipping between the huge boulders, snapped. Just two days on the trail and Adney wrote, "Yesterday a horse deliberately walked over the face of Porcupine Hill." A man who'd seen it told him, "I don't know but that I'd rather commit suicide, too, than be driven by some of the men on this trail." Later Adney reported that there "was at that time no trail but something that they have called a trail, marked by the dead bodies of 3,000 horses."

White Pass Trail became "The Dead Horse Trail," an arduous trail that frayed nerves, turned men to beasts, drove them to brutality, tested their humanity. Some faltered. Some failed. None escaped. Everyone came off the trail changed and some with shame, and ravens circled the ravines to collect the carrion they left behind. Seven miles shy of the summit and seeing enough, Tappan Adney turned back.

By the middle of September the trail had clogged so many times it became impassible. Miners and merchants wrapped handkerchiefs over their noses and pushed the bloated carcasses of dead horses off the ledges into the river, dragged them to the beach for the tide to carry

continued on p. 51

48

— THE DEAD HORSE TRAIL —

ca

Jack London, a young man whose novels *White Fang* and Call of the Wild came out of his experience in the Klondike, was deeply disturbed by the carnage on Dead Horse Trail:

> The horses die like mosquitoes in the frost, and from Skagway to Bennett they rotted in heaps. They died at the rocks, they were poisoned at the summit, and they starved at the lakes; they fell off the trail, what there was of it, and they went through it; in the river they drowned under their loads or were smashed to pieces against the boulders; they snapped their legs in the crevices and broke their backs falling backwards with their packs; in the sloughs they sank from fright or smothered in the slime; and they were disemboweled in the bogs where the corduroy logs turned end up on the mud; men shot them, worked them to death and when they were gone, went back to the beach and bought more. Some did not bother to shoot them, stripping the saddles off and the shoes and leaving them where they fell. Their hearts turned to stone—those which did not break—and they became beasts, the men on the Dead Horse Trail.

Jack Newman, a packer once confessed: "I must admit, I was as brutal as the rest, but we were all mad—mad for gold, and we did things that we lived to regret."

DEAD HORSES ALONG SKAGWAY RIVER
University of Washington Libraries, Special Collections: HEGG 3101

— NOT ALL WERE BUTAL —

❧

Not all who travelled the Dead Horse Trail succumbed to inhumanity. Among them was Harriet Pullen, a vivacious red-head who introduced herself to Skagway as a widow—although she'd left behind in LaPush, WA, a husband, four children and seven horses. She landed September 12, 1897, with $7 in her pocket. Grabbing her valise and scrabbling ashore, she was sitting on a log feeling lost in the crude crowd of ill-mannered miners when suddenly a voice of command called for a cook.

Captain Moore needed a cook for his workers. He gave her the job at $3 a day and showed her a large tent equipped with a sheet metal stove, table, and benches. Boxes lined the walls, dirty dishes sat in heaps, food scraps littered the floor. Eighteen were expected for dinner, but with so many ham shoulders and bacon slabs hanging from the ridgepole she could hardly stand. What's a woman to do? She sat down and had a good cry, then set to work.

Needing more than $3 a day, Harriet scrounged for discarded tin cans and flattened them to make pie tins, then baked dried apple pies late into the night to hawk them for a pretty price come morning. By Christmas she could afford to send for two of her four children and husband. He went to work as a handyman, she continued to bake, making enough pies, she said, "to cover the trail from the middle of the town to the top of the pass." By spring she had enough money to bring up her other children and horses, and straightaway went into freighting. She'd load a four-horse wagon and drive it to the trail foot, then transfer the goods to the backs of her horses and carefully lead them up. At the top, she unloaded, collected her price, then went back for another load. Two years she travelled the Dead Horse Trail—without a single horse lost.

HARRIET PULLEN IN LATER YEARS
by the Author/from a photograph

off, built bridges over the worst. For the miners, every hour counted, every minute. If they didn't get up the trail and over the mountains, it would be too late. They'd be stuck on the wrong side of the mountain range, unable to get to the Klondike until spring—and by then the gold would be gone. For the merchants, it was a race against time as well. The *Dyea Trail* had begun trumpeting her advantages. Finally, at last. The trail reopened. And miners swarmed up White Pass like lunatics!

But new danger prevailed—Soapy's con men. Dr. Kelly (who pioneered the field of gynecology and became a founder of Johns Hopkins Hospital) wrote: "The most prominent feature of the landscape is the activity of the shell-game men and their cappers. How any one can be deceived by these crooks is a mystery....They look evil, and are evil. Great numbers lose heavily and a good many have had to give up their journey and turn back, all funds being lost."

Such men spilled back into Skagway in all sorts of funk. The end of September a huge man in a red shirt sat on the beach sobbing. No money to go on, no money to go home, he and others like him had discovered themselves destitute, forced to sell what remained of their outfits for a pittance to the steady stream of hopefuls arriving daily, too green to comprehend the difficulties ahead—although the exhausted horses standing on the beach in all manner of misery, "For Sale" signs hanging off their necks, might have served caution. But for the incoming *cheechakos,* despite the drenching rain and unabashed tears of the huge man in a red shirt, it was upward and onward in a halo of optimism.

Cheechakos like Leonard Ballard and his partners scrabbled and sloshed through the drizzle. Their optimism soon gave way, though, to worry over frequent delays. Where the trail narrowed, accidents trapped them for hours, leaving them to shiver and grow sick in the misty gloom, their exhausted horses immobilized under crushing loads. Unwilling to remove even a pound lest movement suddenly resume, Ballard's group lost three of their four horses before reaching White Pass City fourteen miles away. The fourth went lame in the Canyon. Something had to be done. If Skagway wanted miners streaming up her troubled trail, she needed a miracle.

They got their miracle unexpectedly in the form of George Brackett.

Brenda Wilbee

Brackett's Road

Former mayor of Minneapolis and a supplier and transporter for the Pacific Northwest Railroad—and ten years contracted with the Great Northern and Canadian Pacific—George Brackett had lost his shirt in the Panic of 1893. With a view to making money like every other Tom, Dick, and Harry—selling goods to miners hellbent on getting to the Klondike—he sent to Skagway twenty-one-year-old Jim (one of seven sons) with a shipment of sheep, beef cattle, hardware, poultry, milch cows, and a plethora of items that could be sold for top dollar. He himself arrived in September with nothing more on his mind than recouping the worst of his losses when fate intervened, altering his destiny—and Skagway's.

On the steamer coming up the coast he'd met a lawyer and former congressman who'd seen the sorry state of White Pass Trail and been pondering the notion of cutting a wagon road along the mountainside, over the pass, and on to Lake Bennett. Would Bracket take charge of such an enterprise? he asked.

Reluctant at first, Brackett finally agreed, and on October 13 he turned his trading post over to son Jim and signed paperwork with thirteen other men that would galvanize a discouraged Skagway with new mettle. Thirteen would prove to be an unlucky number.

BRACKETT'S ROAD
University of Washington Libraries,
Special Collections: HEGG 676

That October, while the Mounties were reporting Skagway a "fair-sized town with well-laid out streets," Dyea was building a two-mile wharf atop their tide flats for easier off-loading. Skagway needed to one-up them. A hastily elected *ad hoc* city council gave Brackett and his partners a right of way through town.

Skagway: It's All About The Gold

November 8th they started. Four days later Brackett had seventy-five employees working at different points along the new route, sticking to the river's east bank. Two weeks from start date, he had four miles of the valley floor finished. Wagon and carts rumbled over the corduroy. Horses clipclopped along. Another fifty men were hired, the road coming together in sections. Bunkhouses were built, one at the summit, another at White Pass City—a cluster of tented hotels and restaurants fifteen miles up the valley where the river veered east. But then a story of woe and grievance. One by one the partners dropped out, or absconded with money, or lined their pockets—or all three and left Brackett holding the bag. Riddance to rubbish was his characteristically optimistic take. Happily he carried on. By mid-December he had 200 employees, eight miles of continuous road, seven camps, and hope of reaching the summit by February 1, 1898.

But by Christmas he was broke.

An appeal to friends in high places included James Hill, an American railroad baron behind the Northern Pacific, and Sir William Van Horne of the Canadian Pacific. Both came through with front money and in March—right about the time Soapy declared himself the uncrowned king of Skagway and Frank Reid's Committee of 101 had posted their futile notice requiring "objectionable characters" to leave town—the various road sections between Skagway and White Pass City were connected. A happy day. Except that when Brackett posted notice that his now fifteen-mile road was officially open and now required a toll—$1/person, $1/pack, and 24¢ a dog—all hell broke lose. Freighters accustomed to free hauling and stampeders thinking the road a God-given right refused to pay and overran his toll gates.

Again Brackett appealed to friends in high places, this time Washington, D.C., and soon the road was

paying out $1,000 to $5,000 a day. He continued up the pass and the miners, bent in winter's wind—and now toiling through driving snow—were moving again.

"Traffic was so great," Roy Minter wrote, that "the whole summit was an unruly tangle of supplies and equipment. Strings of horses and knots of men trudged their way through a sea of frozen slush stained with manure and mud."

On both trails, winter was unspeakably harsh. Stinging gusts came screaming off the passes, driving the swirling, blinding snow into every crevice and crack. The ravines softened, boulders disappeared, snowdrifts piled up ten feet, twenty feet, storm after storm. The mountains literally rose while the trails, packed hard as granite by the tramp of hundreds, came to resemble, as one teenager described Brackett's Road coming out of White Pass City, a pipeline.

Burdened men moved painfully, "leminglike," wrote Pierre Berton—burdened by tents, tools, cooking utensils, burdened by "lime juice and lard, black tea and chocolate, salt, candles, rubber boots and mincemeat, dried potatoes and sauerkraut, string beans and cornmeal, cakes and toilet soap and baking powder, coal oil, lamp chimneys, rope, saws, files, mukluks, overshoes..." Burdened, they used dogs, pack-horses, sleighs, their own backs, and burdened, they parsed their ton of goods into manageable chunks. They tramped five miles before caching their goods and returned for more, over and over, higher and higher, the bitter wind whistling in their ears, threatening frostbite. Back and forth, more snow falling, caches disappearing, frantic shoveling. *Gone!* Burdened, frozen, they'd hurl their frustration and fear at the their dogs, their oxen, their nearly dead horses. One man, after finally crossing the summit, "uncoiled like a steel spring," wrote Pierre Berton, "and in his rage beat his dogs so unmercifully that they could go no farther." He dragged them one by one to an ice-hole and pushed them in, whimpering. In the final silence the man came to his senses and, undone by his dark cruelty, he threw himself into the snow bank and wept. Another man, crazed, built a fire under oxen too exhausted to go on. When they didn't budge, he poked them with burning brands. Still unable to move them, he roasted the oxen alive while other men, heads bent, paying no mind, tromped on by. Frigid air spilled over the pass like a waterfall. Tears could freeze.

The Chilkoot trail out of Dyea fared better. Four companies had begun building trams to haul goods up the steepest inclines—the most impressive being a tow rope that ran alongside the Golden Stairs, a merciless winter climb of 1,500 steps hacked out of ice and snow, enabling thousands to cross the summit that fall and thousands more as winter wore on.

Dyea scored an even bigger coup when the Mounties switched from using the White Pass to the Chilkoot, and her newspaper was quick to publicize the city's virtues over Skagway's lack of them. "Poor Sister Skagway," the *Trail* lamented, citing Soapy's criminal hold, a waterfront riot, and the deadly outbreak of spinal meningitis. Hugh Wallace, president of the Chilkoot Railroad and Transport Company (a rather hefty name for a mere tram line) accelerated the bluff and bluster when he claimed to shipping lines coming up the coast that he could transport any amount of freight to the Klondike. George Brackett, who actually could, jumped into the fray.

"Through trickery," he wrote to William Van Horne of the Canadian Pacific Railroad, "Wallace secured Canadian government freight, which is now stranded at Dyea, and yet he publishes the fact that the government has adopted the route as the only feasible route to be used." He followed it up with an open letter to Wallace, concluding, "I would like to see you working the line you say is 'now in operation' for...you would then be doing what you have for a long while falsely claimed you were doing."

Wallace wrote back in his own open letter: "Your ill-tempered, gratuitous and unjustifiable attack on me might properly be treated with the contempt which the motive that inspired

GEORGE BRACKETT
by the Author/from a photograph

it deserves....Your shafts of abuse are pointless—your assumptions of truth a farce—your letter a tirade of misrepresentations, which are, in fact, but the senile wailings of a desperate and disappointed old man."

Things were getting personal. But then tragedy struck on the Chilkoot Trail, all but yanking the rope from Dyea's hands in the vicious tug-of-war they played, allowing Skagway to emerge the winner as "Gateway to the Klondike."

The 3rd of April a rumble of snow echoed far back of the ridges and deep in the ravines of Chilkoot Trail. The native haulers and guides dug in their heels: avalanche conditions. The dismissive headed up. At noon, suddenly, loose snow began drifting off the glaciers and within seconds—sleds and sleighs abandoned, dogs yelping—men and women plunged downhill in terror under heavy packs but not fast enough, the avalanche rumbling in a thirty-foot cloud of snow. Twenty minutes later it was over, an eerie silence deafening for those who stood somehow alive and shaking. And then moans and cries rose from beneath their boots, leaking into the silence.

Finally, the air exploded as men galvanized to the task. "Quick! Over here!" "Give me a hand!"

Everywhere frantic men shoveled with mitted hands. Within minutes 1,000 men living at Sheep Camp just up the way arrived on the eerie scene and threw themselves into the effort. Tram workers, packers, everyone who could, joined. Around them air holes began to appear, revealing someone alive thirty feet down. Ears pressed, those on top could hear muffled conversations between relatives and friends sealed below as they called to each other their final and faint goodbyes. One old man prayed and swore and prayed again, his voice growing fainter and fainter as hundreds tore at the snow around him, digging parallel trenches in hope of finding him, anyone, alive before it was too late.

A dozen men pulled J. A. Rines free of his icy tomb. Partners Mueller and Joppe were lifted from their snowy grave, one alive, the other dead. Joppe's sweetheart, seeing his snowy body, flung herself screaming at his frozen form, begging him to come back to her. Inconsolable, beside herself, she feverishly rubbed his arms, his legs, his back; she breathed into his lungs and cried and prayed and cried; and breathed into him again and breathed some more. For three hours

Skagway: It's All About The Gold

she kept it up, sustained only by her manic grief to keep dear Joppe with her—while all around men continued to dig. A woman was hauled up by her feet, hysterical but alive. An ox was found chewing its cud in its own little snow stable. Another handful was saved but four of the rescued died on the surface while those beneath succumbed to the carbon dioxide of their own breathing, putting themselves into a sleep from which they never woke. Joppe, given up for dead by everyone but Miss Woodward, suddenly blinked and opened his eyes. *"Vernie?"*[1]

More than sixty bodies were unearthed and hauled down the mountain to a mass morgue where Soapy's men waited to ransack the victims of their valuables. Collectively, the men and women were buried in a mountain hollow not far from where they'd died. Insult to injury, the spring melt made a lake of their graves. Bodies bobbed to the surface. They had to be reburied and today rest just north of Dyea in a peaceful clearing surrounded by spruce and fern and baby hemlock.

SLIDE CEMETERY
Author photograph

Skagway News was quick to exploit the disaster. *Dyea Trail* returned fire. But then an on-scene Hearst newspaper reporter hastened Dyea's end. Bert Colyer through a series of brazen mishaps and lucky breaks scored the big scoop.

And once published in *San Francisco's Examiner?* Futilely, Dyea countered by headlining talk of a possible railroad. Yet it was Skagway who pulled it off. An international coalition of British, Canadian, and American know-how forged a railroad track up White Pass to Bennett Lake and into the Yukon—Captain Moore's sugarplum dreams at last coming to fruition.

A lucky break for Skagway. A death blow for Dyea.

---

1 Joppe and Vernie did not turn out happily-ever-after. In August, the summer before, Mr. Arthur Joppe had married Katherine Henrietta Reuflei. When the *Dyea Trail* publicized the story, he feigned ignorance of his relationship with Vernie but apparently felt the need to go home and do some explaining. He and his bride had, in time, five children, so I expect the explanation was sufficient.

Brenda Wilbee

Happenstance

Skagway's lucky break actually happened by chance. One week after Dyea's devastating avalanche, British financing, American engineering, and Canadian contracting accidently converged one magical night at the St. James Hotel in downtown Skagway. Sir Thomas Tancrede of London's Close Brothers (a banking firm that had taken over management of Ben and Captain Moores' A&NTWTT) had with him two American engineers. The trio was to determine the feasibility of building Captain Moore's train track up the pass. Tonight they were at odds. Sir Tancrede was of the opinion that a track through the mountains was too difficult. Erastus Hawkins and John Hislop disagreed. Suddenly the door opened—and in walked Michael J. Heney, surveyor of the B.C. portion of Canada's Canadian Pacific Railroad. They had no idea who he was.

What happened next was happenstance, though it was a long time in the making—harking back to the previous decade when Captain Moore first secured the financial backing of the Close Brothers' predecessors and gone into partnership with them under the auspices of the A&NWTT Company. In February of 1898, however, Close Brothers purchased the option to expand development—and were now anxious to push forward on the railroad plans that had so tantalized their predecessors—but which, until January, had been held up because of Washington D.C.

ERASTUS HAWKINS, SIR THOMAS TANCREDE, JOHN HISLOP
by the Author/from photographs

Skagway: It's All About The Gold

It fell to Congress to extend U.S. land laws to Alaska; until it did no one could obtain legal right-of-way to move any kind of freight through federal land—gold or otherwise. Only George Brackett had forged ahead with the rather moxie gamble that possession was nine-tenths of the law. But, finally, on January 21, 1898, Representative Lacey of Montana finally introduced the bill that would bring legal clarity. President McKinley wouldn't sign off until May, but it was game on. The Close Brothers, having taken over financial control of A&NWTT, had their go-to men in Skagway by mid-March. April 10th, they were in discord. The last piece had yet to slip into place—Canada's Mike J. Heney.

Two weeks before, on March 28, 1898, an arctic wind had cut down White Pass as if to flay flesh from bone; and Mike Heney had stood shivering on the ship's bridge with his old friend, Captain O'Brien of the *Utopia*, the two of them braced into the wind's whistle and howl as the ship, engines rumbling, slipped into port. They angled past four freighters and a barge already tied up at the Moores' wharf; and while O'Brien piloted them in, singing "Sweet Rosie O'Grady," longshoremen on the dock hardly looked up as they continued to off-load what looked to be several tons of general merchandise and thousands of feet of lumber. To the starboard, a fourth wharf accommodated smaller ships and scows. Double-teamed horses pulled wagons and drays along the busy docks, passing through what Roy Minter described as "canyons of masts, rigging, funnels, and yardarms, each rocking to its own cadence on a wind-driven tide." Seagulls circled overhead. A dead horse bobbed on the water's surface. "A ragged line of debris and crab grass," wrote Minter, "marked the high tide line and a pall of blue smoke hung over the town, a jumble of soot-stained tents, rough board buildings, log cabins, and canvas-covered lean-tos." Heney took note of the St. James Hotel, its huge, black-and-white sign easily visible— ST. JAMES—anchored atop a rusty, corrugated iron roof. O'Brien recommended it. "Has call bells in each room," he said.

Beyond stood the mountains. Even from this distance, Heney knew that any train track going north would be dictated by the colossal spurs of granite interlocked like so many crooked teeth.

Michael Heney was, in fact, Canada's renowned contractor for the country's only transcontinental railroad, the Canadian Pacific.

Minter described him though the eyes of a colleague who "never ceased to wonder where [Heney] obtained his self-assurance, his sense of command, his intuitive understanding of complex engineering problems and his ability to overcome them." No one, Minter continued, understood Heney's success, only that he was "equipped by his nature, his stamina, and his intellect to move mountains." And of late he'd been wondering why, for all the talk of a railroad in SE Alaska, he shouldn't be the one to build it. He aimed to find out.

Between jobs and no mandate but his own curiosity—and his ears stuffed with first-hand accounts of gold and the challenge of wind and cold and the agonizing climb up these passes—he looked first to Dyea as a port to possibly launch his railroad. Without trudging a mile up the trail, however, he concluded that Dyea's three wharves still under construction would be of questionable use. Dyea's two miles of tide flats and a shallow waterfront were a further deterrent. Already cargo had backed up badly. In contrast, Skagway's four wharves and deepwater harbor could receive, sort, and distribute whatever came in. George Brackett, not Hugh Wallace, Heney decided, had the better understanding of the situation. And so he turned his full attention to White Pass.

But if others were cowed by these mountains, he had to ask himself, *could* he *push through?*

He'd done it before, of course, in the Canadian Rockies, but at virtually every point in his inspections between Skagway and Lake Bennett over the next two weeks he saw multiple construction problems. Winter posed even harsher challenges. Temperatures would fluctuate between zero and fifty below. Winter's long hours of darkness, the deep snow and cruel winds would most certainly exact a price. Too, the complexities of overcoming steep grades and narrow gorges and traversing from sea level to the summit in just twenty-one miles—a climb of 3,300 feet through a temperate rain forest into the subalpine and finally arctic tundra—could easily demand twice the budget of any similar railroad built elsewhere. Yet despite these obstacles he returned to Skagway late in the evening of April 10, 1898, bone weary and covered in mud, his clothes tattered and torn, but convinced he could do it. All he needed was money from financiers—with deep pockets and unfettered faith.

Skagway: It's All About The Gold

Where was he to find such men? he wondered, rattling off a few names in his head as he approached Broadway in the growing darkness, amazed by the mud and snow and noisy knots of men gathered at the swinging doors of gambling halls, and the bawling of packers as they swatted the rumps of their horses and mules, cursing a load and getting heated up over a slipped cinch, and hookers sliding out of the shadows to call, "Hey, doll face, ya'll want a good time?" *Which street was St. James on again?* he wondered, tripping over a crate.

St. James Hotel boasted iron-sheeted walls—and advertised itself in the newspapers as Skagway's only fireproof hotel. But its walls were not insulated and tonight April's sudden cold spell infiltrated. "Strategically placed Yukon stoves, their black chimneys supported by a maze of heat-blackened wires, offered the only sources of heat," Minter wrote. And sitting around a polished table in the bar, drawn close to one of the blazing stoves, Tancrede, Hawkins, and Hislop were still deep in dram and debate. They'd been up the pass. They'd created new surveys. They'd gone over the reports. Tancrede summed up the issues, the least of which was the instability of the rock face on the east side of the river. "I'm inclined, gentlemen, to leave the railroad to fools. No, wait," he cautioned, for Hawkins had pushed forward in his chair to

St. James Hotel, Fourth and State
by the Author/from a photograph

argue the point. "Any removal of the slope toe," Tancrede insisted, "is apt to bring avalanches of slide rock from above. You know it'll plague construction and substantially add to our costs."

Sir Tancrede was a man to heed. He'd been senior contractor for the Firth of Forth Bridge, and as a consultant he'd been involved with the construction of several railways in Southeastern United States, Mexico, Mozambique, and Turkey. He'd won awards for his work. It was *his* report London would heed.

The Americans, however, disagreed; and they were not without merit. "If we build on the *west* side," Hislop argued, "the granite there is firmly in place."

"But then we've got the impossible grade," Tancrede reminded him. And so it was. Around and around.

Warm yellow light from two electric bulbs and a kerosene lamp began to cast soft shadows over the table and up the walls. Somewhere the tinkle of honky-tonk could be heard. A gunshot rang out. Two. The night grew late. The hurried slap of running feet outside the window swept by. Another gunshot. Closer this time. The men's discussion lengthened. The contents of their bottle in the middle of the table fell low. Finally, Tancrede flicked the ash off his Havana cigar, swallowed the remains of his drink, and rose stiffly from his chair. He was, after all, fifty-eight years old. "I'm going to bed."

The younger men rose with him.

"I'll sleep on it," Tancrede told them. "I'll let you know in the morning what I'll put in my report to London."

The trio made their way to the desk to pick up their keys, paying little attention to the mud-encrusted man who'd come in and was asking for his own key before dragging himself up the steep, narrow stairs.

"Who's the stranger, Davis?" Hawkins asked absentmindedly of the night clerk, more to make conversation than anything else.

"Mike Heney. The Irish Prince."

"The Irish Prince, you say?"

"He's the one what rammed the CPR through the Rockies. Guess the Canadians think mighty high of the chap."

Hawkins stared up the empty stair case. Was it possible this Mike Heney knew something they didn't? Information that might somehow

Skagway: It's All About The Gold

sway Tancrede? Weeks of surveying, talking, arguing... Hawkins was getting edgy, tense. He hated to quit too soon.

"Says he wants to build a railway outta Skagway," said Davis.

"You don't say."

"Been up at the pass. And out to Bennett, too. Though he probably ain't so keen," offered Davis with a grin, "now's he's seen the pass for hisself."

Again Hawkins stared up the empty stairway "Mr. Davis," he mused to the night clerk, "would you mind asking this man if he'd mind joining us for a drink?"

Tancrede and Hislop both cast Hawkins a queried look.

"He might know something we don't," said Hawkins defensively *and* with a nonchalant shrug.

And thus the convergence of British financing, American engineering, and Canadian contracting. The quartet talked into the wee hours, making music of their collective notes.

MICHAEL J. HENEY
by the Author/from a photograph

Finally Tancrede put it to Heney straight, "Can you build us a railroad?"

"Gentlemen," Heney is purported to have said, leaning back in his chair and offering his famous half smile. "Give me enough dynamite and snoose, I'll build you a railroad to hell."

The White Pass and Yukon Route

Tancrede headed back to London; Hawkins to the Chicago office, Heney to Seattle. Only Hislop remained, and while the others had their own agendas to get the ball rolling, Hislop's was to establish a base camp north of town; in town, a temporary office for the new White Pass and Yukon Route, immediately known as the WP&YR.

Brenda Wilbee

The month wound to a close even as tension mounted around the world. President McKinley finally ordered Spain to withdraw from Cuba. Spain responded by handing the U.S. ambassador his passport, pretty much a declaration of war. McKinley called for volunteers on April 25th, and in Skagway, Soapy Smith wrote to the Secretary of State offering his "militia." All over the Lower 48, men hurried to their nearest recruiting offices. The Spanish-American War was on. In London, Mr. Close hesitated. *Would the WP&YR get mired in the war? Would there be enough ships to transport supplies?* Yet dare he stop?

Twenty other companies had petitioned Canada and the U.S. to build a tram, road, or train to the Yukon—including George Brackett. On the 2nd of May, Mr. Close's American partner in Chicago—Sam Graves, now president of the WP&YR—told Hawkins to go ahead and submit formal application to Washington D.C. for the right-of-way through White Pass. On the 14th of May, President McKinley signed the Homestead Act, extending land laws to Alaska. Mr. Close decided to move ahead and telegraphed Graves, and ordered him to proceed. Graves dispatched Hawkins to Seattle and leapfrogged a telegraph to Heney, ordering *him* to proceed. Proceed Heney did.

Into the holds of two ships, the *City of Seattle* and *Utopia,* went hundreds of tons of timber and dynamite, blasting powder, steel rails, ties, and enough material for three railway stations and a roundhouse. On deck were 100 hired hands. When Hawkins (with his newly chosen WP&YR superintendant Mr. Whiting) arrived into Seattle, all three boarded the *City of Seattle*—and both ships steamed north to Skagway. The whole thing had taken Heney five days to pull off.

They arrived Thursday, May 26th, only to discover they had a sticky issue on their hands—a right-of-way through town.

By necessity, the train track had to run from the Moores' wharf up through town. The logical place was along Skagway's eastern bluff where the dock let out—land Captain and Ben Moore claimed was theirs and which Close Brothers had assumed was theirs as well. *Land,* they were now learning, *the city merchants had usurped and were suing the Moores for. Land squatters had taken over—deadbeats the city refused to oust.* North of town, the situation was no better. Brackett refused to sell his right-of-way.

Skagway: It's All About The Gold

MOORES' SAWMILL, SKAGWAY IN BACKGROUND, AUGUST 1897
by the Author/from a photograph

"A fine kettle of fish," Heney told his new colleagues. Such tangled property rights would keep them in court for years. In the meantime, they had a railroad to build.

Their only real option was to ask the city for a temporary right-of-way down Broadway, the widest street in town, then run the track across the river at Twenty-Third Avenue to the "Foot of the Hill"—then recross the river to a point where they could build above Brackett's Road—*if* the east side proved the better route. But a *train* chug-chugging up through town? Disrupting traffic, spewing dust, smoke, throwing off sparks? To say nothing of the noise and danger to pedestrians crossing the road? People objected. The merchants, too. They'd spent good money on Broadway's lucrative lots and weren't about to let a British railroad company threaten their revenue and real estate.

"First," argued Mr. Cheney, a Broadway clothing merchant, "the street is too narrow for business *and* a railroad, and second, when we are able to obtain insurance in Skagway, the fact that there is a railroad on Broadway will cause rates to be higher on this street than anywhere else in the city."

Mrs. Harrison of Broadway's Ladies' Bazaar said that she was "satisfied that the road on Broadway will be an injury to property owners."

The city council voted to go ahead, anyway, with the right-of-way; and though the paperwork was not yet signed, Heney in good faith ordered the initial tracks laid, up near the river bridge a mile and a half north of town. Hawkins and Hislop headed up the pass to examine both sides of the river—before making a final decision as to which side.

When they returned two weeks later on June 13th, they discovered that the city had retracted on the right-of-way. Heney had hired every horse and man he could find, but now everyone was standing around, twiddling their thumbs. On the beach sat 175 tons of fifty-six-pound rail, lumber, and spikes—with another ship due in any day bearing heavy trestles, powder, more steel rails, bridge piles, a massive three million feet of lumber. A stormy debate broke out that night in the council chamber and dragged on into the night, all the old objections raised again.

"Once you let them on the street, they'll never get off!"

Superintendant Whiting reiterated it was only for year, until negotiations could be made for the east side. "And you've already agreed," he reminded the Council. "We made plans accordingly."

The Council stalled, asked for a twenty-four-hour delay. It would give the Broadway merchants, they said, time to buy out the squatters on the east side. Reluctantly, the WP&YR agreed, but when the next night complications were reported, Superintendent Whiting lost patience. "The time for talk is over! We must have immediate action!" He walked out. His thinly veiled threat of moving over to Dyea not lost on anyone. Just after midnight he heard a knock on his door. A few councilmen stood on his stoop, twisting their hats. "The majority will sign off come morning," they promised.

Unwilling to take the chance and wait for signatures, Whiting ordered Heney to begin immediately. In the dark hours before dawn, then, Heney put 100 men to work, staking the grade down Broadway. By seven o'clock in the morning, he had 500 men leveling the grade. Stunned Broadway merchants woke to *fais accomplis*.

"A serious blow," summed up J. G. Price—representing the Broadway merchants against the railroad. Joseph Burkhard of Burkhard Hotel and Hardware gave voice to his feelings through Councilman Lokowitz—who had *not* voted for the right-of-way and wanted everyone to know it.

Skagway: It's All About The Gold

RAILROAD TRACK DOWN BROADWAY, LOOKING SOUTH
by the Author/from a photograph

      The property owners on Broadway have been shamefully used after all the expense they have gone to in improving the street. Besides, the railroad will necessarily drive all retail business away from it, as people are afraid to risk their lives by running around locomotives and trains. The value of property on other streets will be enhanced at the expense of Broadway. I have opposed putting the track along Broadway, both as a citizen and as a councilman, and I very much regret the fact that my efforts in that direction were unavailing.

      A Broadway tobacco shop owner was more disgusted than angry. "I don't care a hell of a lot about it," he said. "Still, it makes me hot to see the street torn up that way." Mr. Peoples, the undertaker, summed it up for pretty much everyone else: "What's the use of kicking. Let 'er go."

      It would take two years, two months, and two days to build the track from Skagway to Whitehorse in the Yukon 110 miles away—a narrow-gauge rail bed winding up the mountains just as Captain Moore had anticipated, skirting the Trails of '97 and '98, running above Brackett's Road, 3,000 dead horses in shadow and shale, and climbing from sea level to 3,300' in twenty miles. Tunnels, bridges, trestles, 16° turns, 4% grades, rock faces so steep men had to rappel and work in suspension, temperatures 60 below, 450 tons of black powder, 35,000 workers, only 35 deaths. July 29, 1900, President Sam Graves from the Chicago office, in the Yukon to celebrate, sledge-hammered the golden spike into place at Carcross, Yukon. An engineering feat.

Two years, two months, and two days.

By then the "easy" gold was gone. The average Joe—with not much more than a gold pan, pick and a shovel—had moved on to Atlin, B.C. and Nome, AK, leaving the Klondike to commercial dredging. But no one in Skagway much cared. She'd gained ascendancy. She, not Dyea, had won the title "Gateway to the Klondike." And her economic survival was now guaranteed. As a railroad town—and as a Canadian port on American soil—she was shipping Yukon silver, copper, and iron all over the world—and, world over, drawing more and more tourists to ride her rails up the White Pass Trail, haunted still, and adventures beyond.

The first tourists arrived in 1898. The first flyer went out in 1902. Today a million tourists visit Skagway every summer.

Would one of them be you?

PASSENGERS ON THE WP&YR
by the Author/from a photograph

It's All About The Gold
Without the gold, there'd be no Skagway.

Skagway: It's All About The Gold

Yet Skagway never had gold—only an uncanny knack for creating it off every fool and dreamer who went after it. Captain Moore and his son certainly made their fortunes. After the court initially ruled against them in the lawsuit filed on their behalf by the A&NWTT against the city for its usurpation of their homestead, an appeal won them back sixty of their 160 acres. By January of 1900, however, taking over ownership of everyone's businesses would seriously hamper the city—and the Moores, as well as the A&NWTT and Close Brothers, realized that prudence was the better part of valor. In September 1900, then, they reached a compromise with the effected businessmen: They'd settle for 25% of the merchants' assessed value. A few refused to pay, closed up shop, and left town. Andrew Barr wrote:

> One day we received a report from the Department of the Interior in Washington that the town site of Skagway was properly and legally owned by Captain William Moore and his son Ben. This report created another panic in the business section and I saw that I must engage in mining altogether or return to my home in L.A.

For those who stayed and paid, it was a sizable chunk of change for the Moores. Too, the wharf (described by Ben as the goose that laid the golden egg) netted handsome profits. Their sawmill brought in its own a small fortune. And when Captain Moore left Skagway for good in 1906, he sold his interest in the WP&YR for $125,000. A conservative estimate today would be $3,000,000.

George Brackett did equally well, eventually selling his right-of-way and wagon road to the WP&YR for $110,000. Today's value? $2,640,000.

As to the Close Brothers, their WP&YR cost ten million dollars to build, but their investment paid back before the track was finished and today continues to realize a fantastic profit—as a passenger train. Back in 1994, the WP&YR was declared an International Historic Civil Engineering Landmark—kudos to Michael J. Heney for his ability "to move mountains"—sharing the honor with the Eiffel Tower, Statue of Liberty, and Panama Canal. A little known fact is that the WP&YR invented the container car method of transportation. Next time you see a box car snapped onto a long-haul flatbed, remember it was the WP&YR that started it. Finally, in 1951, after more than half a century, Close Brothers sold to Canadian investors, and today Close Brothers are the U.K.'s largest independent merchant bank—and one of the top 200 companies on the London Stock Exchange. They did not do badly.

As to the early Skagway merchants, they made their money and moved on. Others stayed. Some of the early families—like the Dedmans, who still run the Dedman's Photo Shop and Art Gallery—did very well indeed.

DEDMAN'S
Author photograph

In the Klondike itself, prospectors already in the area when Skookum Jim found the gold obviously took the lion's share. The first haul to come out of the Interior in July 1897—triggering the headlines of GOLD! GOLD! GOLD! GOLD!—amounted to more than two million dollars. In 1898, between July and November the U.S. Mints in Seattle and San Francisco received *ten* million. By 1900, *thirty-eight* million. By 1902/1903, commercial dredging moved in and millions more came out of the earth. Dredge #4 was as tall as an eight-story building—and it crawled the riverbeds, digging up the ground seventy-five feet down; and today all along the Klondike River and its tributaries the earth lies a stony rubble turned upside down and inside out.

Dredging is no longer legal for obvious reasons, but now the *hills* are being torn down, sifted through, and bull-dozed back into place—minus flora and fauna. Such land "reclamation" satisfies a legal requirement but can't possibly translate into reality. But as long as there's "gold in them thar hills," *and there is*, people will find ways to go after it. To date, more than 2 million ounces have been taken out. At $1600 an ounce, it multiplies out to $32 billion dollars—with no end in sight.

So what about every fool and dreamer who went after it with just their pick and pan more than a hundred years ago? One might ask first about Skookum Jim who, with his nephew Dawson Charlie and brother-in-law George Carmack, discovered the gold only days after Bob Henderson had insulted him, refusing to sell any "damn Siwash" a plug of

Skagway: It's All About The Gold

tobacco. By 1900, Jim had purchased George Carmack's *and* Dawson Charley's interests—and 1904, when he the claims to Lewes River Mining and Dredging Company for $65,000, he'd already made millions in today's currency. Henderson, it's said, never forgave Jim *or* Cormack. Not that either man minded. Jim continued to mine in Atlin, B.C. and Nome, AK, garnering the admiration of men like William Ogilvie, Canada's Dominion Surveryor, while he enjoyed the lavish lifestyle of a *very* rich white man. When he wasn't prospecting, Jim wore a tailored suit and white shirt, with a heavy gold nugget watch-chain draped across his vest—and a large nugget stickpin in his tie. And when George abandoned Kate for the questionable Marguerite of Dawson City (leaving Kate and their daughter Graphie Gracie destitute), Jim built his sister and niece a home in Carcross, Yukon. He also built his wife and daughter Daisy a nearby home—rumored to have cost $20,000, an astronomical sum in those days. He spared no expense, purchasing lumber in SE Alaska, shipping it by rail to Bennett, floating it to Carcross, and then installing a brass bedstead, a gramophone, elaborately carved furniture—including a dining room table made with gold nuggets inlaid into the chairs. He traveled too in search of the exotic, bringing home a Persian rug and chandelier. At some point he created a $20,000 trust for Daisy. In his will, he made provision for Kate. The bulk of his estate, however, he put into trust for "deserving Indians...in any way or manner said trustees may deem best," providing also for "furnishing medical attendance supplying necessities and comforts." Today in Whitehorse, capital of the Yukon, the Skookum Jim Friendship Center continues to finance similar programs—gold rush money well spent.

George Carmack, his brother-in-law—traditionally given credit for having found the gold—also took in millions, if we're to use today's currency. For a man who wanted nothing more in life than to be native, George—once he struck it rich—decided he liked being a white man after all. He dumped his Tagish Princess, Kate, and took up with one of Dawson City's madams, Marguerite, owner of the Green Apple Cigar Shop—a brothel. By all appearances, it was a good match. George and Marguerite retired to Seattle where they dabbled in real estate and did well for themselves.

Brenda Wilbee

ADVENTURE AND CAMARADERIE
Alaska State Library: Winter and Pond Collection, ASL-P21-17

But what of the others, the million worldwide who dreamed and schemed and of the 100,000 who actually set out? The losers who made nothing, men like Montgomery Hawthorne, William Haskell, Ezra Meeker, and Lillian Oliver? Only 40,000 of them ever made it to Dawson City. Of the 40,000, only 400 struck it rich. Of the 400, only 40, give or take, managed to hang onto it. One is John Nordstrom; and we know what *he* did with his money. Ever hear of Donald Trump? Where the Chilkoot and White Pass Trails converged in Bennett City, his great-grandfather built a hotel and raked in a fortune. The hotel is no longer there, but his fortune still headlines the news. *The others? The other 39,960?* It's interesting, in the diaries and memoirs left behind, men and women wrote in glowing terms of the gold they'd find and how wonderful life would be when they found it. But by the end, we read instead of friendships and adventure, of lessons learned, of richness in their lives — something gold could never have bought. Very few, it seems, regretted giving it all up. Perhaps they weren't the losers after all.

Welcome to Skagway

But nothing's changed in Skagway. It's still all about the gold. Instead of selling bacon and beans to every miner coming into town,

72

Skagway: It's All About The Gold

Skagway sells diamonds and trinkets to every tourist who walks off a cruise ship. Yes, Skagway is *still* all about the gold. The truth is, without the gold Skagway would not exist. She exists on your dime. Make no mistake. But this doesn't mean she aims to hoodwink you into some kind of scam or fleece you of your grubstake—like Soapy Smith surely would. Skagway's merchants and vendors instead offer what the gold miners discovered—adventure. They do this in spades because Skagway is still Gateway to the Klondike, a narrow portal through which people enter to cross the White Pass and into the vista beyond. More people than ever tie up at her docks and come ashore, enlivened by the seductive scent of discovery that continues to lift off the cliffs and waft up the valley. Some strap on their backpacks, knot their Nikes, and head for the hills—Lower Dewey Trail, Reid Falls, Smuggler's Cove, AB Mountain; others check for passports and camera and climb aboard the historic White Pass & Yukon train (WP&YR); still others hop helicopters, clamber onto motor coaches, or rent a car to explore the nearby glaciers and Dead Horse Trail of the Klondike Gold Rush. Many, like Frank Reid in 1897, find the city of sufficient interest to stay put. Whatever your adventure, it all begins in Skagway.

ALEAH SPRINGSNOW LORENZ
Author photograph

Welcome!

Brenda Wilbee

Skagway: It's All About The Gold

Bibliography

Adney, Tappan. The Klondike Stampede. 1900. Introduction Ken Coates.
Vancouver, BC: UBC Press, 2003.

"Alaska Goldrush National Historic Landmarks: The Stampede North."
National Parks Service. 9 January 2011. <www.nps.gov/akso/CR/
AKRCultural/ CulturalMain/3PDF/Goldrush.pdf

Allen, J Sidna. Memoirs of J Sidna Allen: A True Narrative of What Really
Happened At Hillsville, Virginia. Mt. Arry, Carolina.

Allen, June. "Alaska-Canada Boundary Dispute(s): Who Drew the Lines and
Why." Sit News. 22 April 2003. 9 November 2011. < http://www.sit-
news.net/JuneAllen/Border/042203_ak_ca_border.html>

Association of Ontario Land Surveyors. "William Ogilvie." Alberta's Land
Surveying Association. 11 November 2010. http://www.landsurveyin-
ghistory.ab.ca/Characters/Ogilvie_W.htm

Bachelder, Lesse A. "Diary of Lesse A. Bachelder, Year 1898: Klondike
God Rush British Yukon Territory." Vertical File, Klondike Gold Rush
National Historic Park Archive.

Ballard, Lanning. Vertical File, Klondike Gold Rush National Historic Park
Archive.

"Banking on the Stampeders: Dyea vs. Skagway." Postal Museum. 8 January
2011. <http:www.postalmuseum.si.edu/gold/skagdyea.html>

Banon, Edward Magawley. The Diary of Edward Magawley Banon, Esq.
A.I.M.E: Kondike British Yukon. Ward Printing Co. Rhode Island,
1948.

Barr, Andrew Lloyd. "Marvelous Adventures of Three Gold Seekers in Alaska."
Vertical Files, Klondike Gold Rush National Historic Park Library.

Barton, Everett. Letter, 8/27/1897. Vertical Files, Klondike Gold Rush
National Historic Park Library.

Beares, Frank G. Letter to mother, 4, 6th 1898. Vertical Files, Klondike Gold
Rush National Historic Park Library.

Bearss, Edwin C. and White, Bruce M. "George Brackett's Wagon Road."
Minnesota History Magazine. Minnesota Historical Society. 9 January
2011. <http://www.google.com/search?q=George+Brackett&ie=utf-8-
&oe=utf-8&aq=t&rls=org.mozilla:en-US:official&client=firefox-a>

Brenda Wilbee

Berry, Caleb. 1898. Vertical Files, Klondike Gold Rush National Historic Park Library.

Beaty, James. Manuscript. Verticle File, Skagway's National Gold Rush Historic Park Library.

Berton, Pierre. Klondike: The Last Great Gold Rush, 1896-1899. Anchor Canada Paper Back Edition; Division of Random House. 1972.

_____. The Great Klondike Gold Rush. Fifth House. Calgary. 2007.

Borneman, Walter R. Alaska: Saga of A Bold Land, From Russian Fur Traders to the Gold Rush, extraordinary railroads, WWII, the oil boom, and the fight over the Arctic National Wildlife Refuge. New York: HarperCollins, 2003.

Brady, Jeff. "Skagway, Alaska: Gateway to the Klondike/Gold Rush 1897. Skagway Convention Center and Visitors Bureau. 22 January 2011. <http://www.skagway.com/history.html>

Brown, Wayne F. Steele's Scouts: Samuel Benfield Steel and the North-West Rebellion. Heritage House. Surrey, BC, 2001.

Campbell, Stewart Lawrence (Jan 26/1898 – Aug 29/1899). Verticle File, Skagway's National Gold Rush Historical Park Library.

"Canadian Mounties in History and Literature." 11 January 2911. North-West Mounted Police. <http://www.mounted-police.00books.com>.

"Carcross Historic Buildings: Walking Tour." YTG CulturalServices Branch Brochure.

Carter, Charles W. "Alaska Gold Rush" Oral History. Vertical File. Klondike Gold Rush Historic Park Library.

Chambers, Captain Ernest J, The Royal North-West Mounted Police: A Corps History. Mortimer Press: Montreal, 1906.

"Committee of 101." Legends of America: A Travel Site for the Nostalgic & Historic Minded. 21 August 2011. <http://www.legendsofamerica.com/we-vigilantelist2.html>.

Cooper, Michael. Klondike Fever: Famous Gold Rush of 1898. Clarion Books. New York, 1989.

Cruise, David and Griffiths, Alison. The Great Adventure: How the Mounties Conquered the West. Penguin Books Canada. Toronto. 1996.

Cyr, Alice. "Stories of Skagway" Oral Histories. Vertical File. Klondike Gold Rush Historic Park Library.

Skagway: It's All About The Gold

Dahl, Robert A. After the Gold Rush: Growing Up In Skagway. Xlibris Corp. 2005.

Daily Alaskan. "Aviator C. O. Prest." June 6, 1922

Daily Alaskan. Special Edition, Jan 1901.

Daily Alaskan. "Summer Tourists Come to Skaguay." July 1898.

Daily Alaskan. "Tony Dortero," January 1, 1901.

Denver Post. 11/27/1989, p 12.

Dickey, R.M, Rev. Gold Fever: A Narrative of the Great Klondike Gold Rush, 1897-1899. Klondike Research: Juneau, AK, 1977,

Driscoll, Cynthia Brackett. One Woman's Gold RUsh: Snapshots from Molie Brackett's Lost Photo Album, 1898-1899. Oak Wood Media. 1966.

Dubuque Daily Herald. Nov 16, 1899. <http://skagwayfolklore.blogspot.com/2011/06/homeward-bound-from-hell-and-mosquitoes.html>

Duncan, Jennifer. Frontier Spirit: The Brave Women of the Klondike. Anchor Canada, Division of Random House. 2004

Dyea Trail. "Avalanche." April 6, 1898.

Dyea Trail. 3/11/1898.

Elsner, Lucille Hudson and Clark, Helen. Interview, Dave Cohen, July 8, 1981. KLGO 45016. Klondike Gold Rush National Historic Park Archives.

Emmets, Katie. "Tall Restoration Order." Skagway News. 23 July 2010. <http://www.skagwaynews.com/072310NPSbuildingRestorationFeature.html

"End of Soapy Smith, Bad Man." The San Francisco Chronicle. July 24, 1898: 17.

Gaffin, Jane. "William Ogilvie: Dominion Surveyor Made Order Out of Chaos." 11 November 2010. PDF web: <http://www.googlecom/url?sa=t&source=web&cd=3&sqi=2&ved=0CC0QFjAC&url=ttp%3A%2F%2Fnorthland.com%2Fpa%2FWilliam%2520Ogilvie.

Garden City, Alaska." Yukon News. 20 January 2011. < http://www.yukon-info.com/skagway/info/gardencity.htm>

Guttman, Jon. "Soapy Smith: Con Man's Empire." History Net. 6/12/2006. 21 January 2011. <http://www.historynet.com/soapy-smith-con-mans-empire.htm/print/>

Hacking, Norman. Captain William Moore: BC's Amazing Frontiersman. Surrey, B.C: Heritage House, 1993.

Hague, Reece. "Ghosts of the Past." unknown magazine. June 1931.

Brenda Wilbee

"Harriet Pullen, Ma." Postal Museum. 14 January 2011. <http://www.postal-museum.si.edu/gold/pullen.html#pullenhouse>

Heilprin, Angelo. Alaska and the Klondie: A Journey to the New3 Eldorado With Hints to the Traveller. D. Appleton & Co. NY, 1903.

"History." Red Onion Saloon. 25 January 2011. <http://www.redonion1898.com/>

Hogben. Interview, 1965. Vertical File. Klondike Gold Rush National Historic Park Library.

Houston, Bonnie. Historic Preservation in Skagway: A Guide to Planning. (M.A. thesis, Arizona State University, 2000)

Horrall, S.W. The Pictorial History of the Royal Canadian Mounted Police. McGraw-Hill Ryerson Ltd. Toronto, 1973.

Hunt, William. Whiskey Trader.

Johnson, Jim Albert. Carmack of the Klondike. Seattle, WA: Epicenter & Horsdal & Schubart, 1990

Johnson, Jim Albert. George Carmack: Man of Mystery Who Set Off The Klondike Gold Rush. Seattle, WA: Epicenter & Harsdal & Shubart, 2001.

Jones, Cherry Lyon. More Than Petticoats: Remarkable Alaskan Women. Morris Book Publishing. 2006 <http://books.google.com/books?id=h eYQFIZsLAAC&pg=PA1&lpg=PA1&dq=Harriet+Pullen&source=bl &ots=1065Z8_dSI&sig=6P21vUaO8RkhtgcQyp-mxg6me5k&hl=en& ei=5Ss2TcjcGYOosAOWmoC4AQ&sa=X&oi=book_result&ct=resu lt&resnum=6&ved=0CEEQ6AEwBTgK#v=onepage&q=Harriet%20 Pullen&f=false>

Kalen, Barbara Dedman. "Stories For Tourists." Verticle Files, Klondike Gold Rush National Historical Park Archives. Skagway, AK.

"Klondike Gold Rush." National Parks Service. 21 January 2011. < http:// www.nps.gov/klgo/planyourvisit/chilkoottrail.htm >

"Klondike 1890s." A Country of Consent: CD-ROM history of Canada. West Dunn Productions. 14 January 2011. <http://www.canadahistoryproject. ca/PDF_En/STUFF/1896.PDF>

LaRouche, Frank. En Route to the Klondike: Chilkoot Pass and Skagway Trail. W.B. Conkey Co. NY, 1897.

Larson, Dennis M. Slick as a Mitten: Ezra Meeker's Klondike Enterprise. Pullman WA: WSU Press, 2009.

Skagway: It's All About The Gold

Ledoux, Gary. "John Clum In Alaska." Tombstone Times. March 2009. 22 October 2011. < http://www.tombstonetimes.com/stories/clum01.html>

Lyon, Robert, Editor. Jeff. Smiths Parlor Museum Historic Structure Report. U.S. Dept of the Interior: National Parks Service Alaska Regional Office. 2010.

McCMan, Couley. "Experiences in Alaska During the Gold Rush: Letter Written by Couley Man in 1897 Re-Printed here." Oscar Belcher Vertical File, Skagway's Gold Rush National Historic Park Library.

McCluskey, Marlene. Skagway Historical Society. 9 November 2011. <http://skagwayfolklore.blogspot.com/2011/05/howard-atwood-kelly.html>

McCluskey, Marlene. Skagway Historical Society. 22 August 2011. <http://skagwayfolklore.blogspot.com/2011/05/alexander-grey.html>

McKeown, Martha Ferguson. The Trail Led North: Mont Hawthorne's Story. New York: MacMillan Co. 1948.

McLaughlin, Les. Hougengroup: Yukon Nuggets. 23 November 2010. <http://www.hougengroup.com_yukonHistoryfactsyear/1880saspx?year880=1840.html>

McLaughlin, Les. "Anton Vogee Klondike Gold Painters." Hougengroup: Yukon Nuggets. 21 October 2011. <http://www.hougengroup.com/yukonhistory/nuggets_year/2000s.aspx?nugget=1950>

McLaughlin, Les. "Diary of Otto Steiner." Hougengroup: Yukon Nuggets. 21 October 2011. <http://www.hougengroup.com/yukonhistory/nuggets_year 2000s.aspx?nugget=1955>

McLaughlin, Les. "Kate Carmack." Hougengroup: Yukon Nuggets. 21 October 2011. <http://www.hougengroup.com/yukonhistory/nuggets_year/2000s.aspx?nugget=1920>

McLaughlin, Les. "Klondike Kate." Hougengroup: Yukon Nuggets. 21 October 2011. <http://www.hougengroup.com/yukonhistory/nuggets_year/2000s.aspx?nugget=1957>

McLaughlin, Les. "Lake Bennett." Haugengroup: Yukon Nuggets. 21 October 2011. < http://www.hougengroup.com/yukonhistory/nuggets_year/2000s.aspx?nugget=1953>

McLaughlin, Les. "Michael Heney" Haugengroup: Yukon Nuggets. 21 October 2011. <http://www.hougengroup.com/yukonhistory/nuggets_year/2000s.aspx?nugget=1910>

Brenda Wilbee

McLaughlin, Les. "White Pass The Container Pioneers." Hougengroup: Yukon Nuggets. 21 October 2011. <http://www.hougengroup.com/yukonhistory/nuggets_year/ 2000s.aspx?nugget=1957>

Miller, Mike. Soapy: Alaska's Most Notorious Outlaw and Con Man. Alaskabooks. Juneau, 1970.

Minor, David. Eagles Byte. 17 January 2011. <http://home.eznet.net/~dminor/ TM000624.html>

Moore, Bernard J. Skagway in Days Primeval: The Writings of J. Bernard Moore 1886-1904. 1908. Forward Donald A. Gestner. Skagway: Lynn Canal Publishing, 1968.

"Mounties and the Klondike Gold Rush of 1898." url.biz. 13 January 2011. < http://www.url.biz/Articles/Article-3318.html>

Morgan, Lael. Good Time Girls of the Alaskan-Yukon Gold Rush. Epicenter. Fairbanks, 1998.

Morning Oregonian. 3/16/1868.

Moxley, Bill and Patti. "Skagway, Alaska—The Gateway to the Klondike." TravelBlog. 14 August 2009. 11 November 1010. <http://www.travelblog.org/North-America/United-States/blog-428847.html>

Murphy, Claire Ruolf and Haigh, Jane G. Gold Rush Women. Alaska Northwest Books. Anchorage, 1997.

National Park Service U.S. Dept of the Interior. "Skagway: Gateway to the Kondike." <http://www.nps.gov/history/nr/twhp/wwwlps/lessons/ 75skagway/ 75skagway.htm>

National Park Service. Golden Places: The History of Alaska-Yukon Mining, Chapter 2. "Interior Riches." <http://www.nps.gov/history/history/online_books/yuch/golden_places/chap2.htm>

Norris, Frank. Legacy of the Gold Rush: An Administrative History of Klondike Gold Rush National Historical Park. Anchorage AK: National Park Service Alaska System Support Office, 2006.

Ogilvie, William. Early Days on the Yukon. 1913. Whitehorse, Yukon: Wolf Creek Classics. 1913.

"Part 1: The Golden Dream. Chapter 1: Skagway, District of Alaska—A Chronology." Klondike Gold Rush Skagway, District of Alaska—1884-1912: Building the Gateway to the Klondike / Historical and Preservation Data. 6 August 2009. 21 August 2011. <http://www.nps.gov/history/history/online_books/klgo/hpd1/chap1.htm>

Skagway: It's All About The Gold

"Part 1: The Golden Dream. Chapter 2: Skagway, District of Alaska—A Historic View." Klondike Gold Rush Skagway, District of Alaska—1884-1912: Building the Gateway to the Klondike / Historical and Preservation Data. 6 August 2009. 21 August 2011. <http://www.nps.gov/history/history/online_books/klgo/hpd1/chap2.htm>

"Part II: Building The Dream. Chapter 3: Archeological Development." Klondike Gold Rush Skagway, District of Alaska—1884-1912: Building the Gateway to the Klondike / Historical and Preservation Data. 6 August 2009. 21 August 2011. <http://www.nps.gov/history/history/online_books/klgo/hpd1/chap3.htm>

Pennington, Gerald L. Klondike Stampeders Register: A Chronology of the Klondike Gold Rush 1897-1898. San Diego, CA: Windsor Assoc. 1997.

Pullen, Harriet. Correspondence Pullen Papers Vert

Pullen, Royal. "Skagway Recollections With His Daughter Ruth Hamilton Pullen." March 1988. KLGO 45017. Klondike Gold Rush National Historic Park Archives.

Rennick, Penny, Editor. Skagway, A Legacy of Gold. The Quarterly, Vol 19, Num 1. Anchorage, AK: Alaska Geographic, 1992.

Richter, Francine. Inteview, Joan Beierly. Vertical File. Klondike Gold Rush Historic Park Library.

Rocky Mountain News. 9/21/1889.

Sauerwein, Stan. Soapy Smith: Skagway's Scourge of the Klondike. Canmore, AL: Altitude Publishing. 2005. Schaller, David T. "Reinventing Skagway." Ecotourism Research and Other Adventures. 29 May 1998. 24 November 2010. <http://www.eduweb.com/schaller/Skagway.html>

Schaller, David T. "Reinventing Skagway." Ecotourism Research and Other Adventures. 29 May 1998. 24 November 2010. <http://www.eduweb.com/schaller/Skagway.html>

Selmer, Oscar. 9/24/1996. Interview. Vertical File. Klondike Gold Rush Historic Park Library.

Sinclair, James M. Mission: Klondike, From Lawless Skagway to Bennett and Dawson. Mitchell Press, Ltd: Canada. 1978.

Singer, Donald L., PhD. "Soapy Smith: Uncrowned King of Skagway." Speech in the Fortnightly Club of Redlaqnds, CA. Jan 2, 2003 9 Nov 2011, <http://www.redlandsfortnightly.org/papers/singer03.htm>

Brenda Wilbee

Sinnwell, Michael. "Skagway Alaska Ghostown." Rocky Mountain Profiles. 5 January 2011.

Sinnwell, Michael. 14 January 2011. <http://www.rockymountainprofiles. com/skagway_alaska.htm>

Skaguay News.

"Skagway Alaska." Bell's Travel Guide. 2 December 2010. <http://www.bell-salaska.com/skagway.html>

"Skagway, Alaska." WordIQ. 29 November 2010. <http://www.rockymoun-tainprofiles.com/skagway_alaska.htm>

Skagway, A Legacy of Gold. Alaska Geographic, Vol 19, N0 1. 1992.

"Skagway Economy." Skagway Development Corporation. 27 June 2011. http://skagwaydevelopment.org/skagwayeconomy.html

Skagway Garden Club. Garden City of Alaska. Skagway, 2003.

"Skagway, Gateway to the Klondike." Teaching with Historic Places Lessons Plans. National Parks Service. 23 November 2010. <http://www.nps.gov/ history/nr/twhp/wwwlps/lessons/75skagway/75skagway.htm>

"Skookum Jim: Packer and Prospector Extraordinaire." Yukon News. 31 March 2010. MacBride Museum. 10 November 2010. <http://www.yu-kon-news.com/opinions/columns/17459

Smith, Jeff. Alias Soapy Smith: The Life and Death of a Scoundrel. Klondike Research: Juneau. 2009.

Smith, Jefferson III. "Skagway Deputy US Marshal James M. Rowan." SoapySmiths.blogspot. 11 August 2010. 9 December 2010. <http.//www. soapysmiths.blogspot.com>.

Smith, Jefferson II. "History I-IV." Alias Soapy Smith. 25 November 2010. 10 December 2010. <http:www//soapysmith.net>

"Soapy Smith: Con Man's Empire." HistoryNet. History Magazine. 1/1/12. <http://www.historynet.com>.

"Some Skagway History." Rocky Mountain Profiles. 13 August 2010. 26 November 2010. <http://www.rockymountainprofiles.com/skagway_alaska.htm>.

Spotwood, Ken. "The History of Carcoss, Yukon Territory." Explore the Yu-kon. 21 October 2011. < http://www.explorenorth.com/yukon/carcross-history.html>

Spude, Catherine Holder, PhD. The Mascot Saloon: Archeological Investiga-tions in Skagway, Alaska. National Park Service, Dept of US Interior. Anchorage, AK, 2006.

Skagway: It's All About The Gold

Spude, Catherine Holder. "That Fiend in Hell" Soapy Smith in Legend. Norman OK: University of Oklahoma Press, 2012.

Spude, Robert L. S. Klondike Gold Rush Skagway, District of Alaska: 1884-1912: Building the Gateway to the Klondike. Klondike Gold Rush Historical Park National Park Service. Skagway.

Steele, Sir Samuel. _____. Herbert Jenkins, Ltd: London, 1935.

_____ . B. C.B. N.V.O. Forty Years in Canada. McClelland & Stewart, Ltd. Toronto. 1914.

Steffa, Don. "Tales of Noted Frontier Characters III: "Soapy" Smith, Bad Man & Bluffer." The Pacific Monthly, October 1908. Vol. XX. No. 4

"Sustainable Skagway." 13 August 2009. Sustainable Skagway. 26 January 1011. <http://www.sustainableskagway.blogspot.com/>

Tower, Elizabeth A. Big Mike Heney: Irish Prince of the Iron Trails: Builder of the White Pass and Yukon and Coppery River Northwest Railways. Anchorage AK, 1988.

University of Washington. Digital Collections. <http://content.lib.washington.edu/heggweb/index.html>

Warmen, Cy. "Building A Railroad Into The Klondike." McLure's Magazine, March 1900.

Weiking, Bob (Martin Itjen's descendent). "Martin Itjen." Wikipedia.org. 28 October 2010. 22 January 2011. <http://en.wikipedia.org/w/index.php?title=Martin_Itjen&printable=yes>

"Welcome to the Municipality of Skagway Borough, Gateway to the Klondike." Gateway to the Klondike Municipality of Skagway. 3 November 2010. 10 December, 2010. <http://www.skagway.org/>

Wells, Steve. High Points of Skagway Sociological Study, Gary Higgins. KLGO 45013. Klondike Gold Rush National Park Archives.

Wieking, Bob. " Yukon Gold Rush-Martin and Lucy Itjen." Wieking der Viking Blog. 9 November 2008. 21 October 2011. <http://wiekingderviking.blogspot.com/search/label/Skaagway>

"White Pass Story." White Pass and Yukon Route. 8 August 2011. <http://www.wpyr.com/history/brochures/Welcome-To-Gold-Rush-07-08.jpg>

Whiting, F. B. MD. Grit, Grief and Gold. Seattle WA: Peacock Publishing Co., 1933.

Brenda Wilbee

"William Moore (steamship captain)." 13 November 2010. 24 November 2010. <http://en.wikipedia.org/wiki/William_Moore_%28steamship_captain%29>

"William Ogilvie." Alberta Land Surveying History. 29 November 2010. <http://www.landsurveyinghistory.ab.ca/Characters/Ogilvie_W.htm>

Williams, D Scott. "Our Alaska Business and People." Mar 1988. Vertical File. Klondike Gold Rush Historic Park Library.

Yukon Alaska Tourist Tours. "Bus/Train Combo." 21 August 2011. < http://www.yukonalaskatouristtours.com/bustrainmoreinfo.html>

Yukon News. "Skookum Jim—Packer and Prospector Extraordinaire." Yukon News. < http://www.yukon-news.com/opinions/columns/17459/>

Yukon Tourism & Industry. "Venus Mill: John Conrad's Jewell." <http://www.yukonalaskatouristtours.com/bustrainmoreinfo.html>

Zane, Willis Albert. Vertical File. Klondike Gold Rush Historic Park Library.

Skagway: It's All About The Gold

Author Bio

BrendaWilbee.com
Brenda@BrendaWilbee.com

Brenda Wilbee is a feature writer and award-winning author of twelve instructional seminars and ten books with over 700,000 copies sold in the US, Canada, Europe, and the U.K. She received her MA at Western Washington University, taught college composition for seven years, and is a frequent speaker at writers conferences, press conventions, elder hostels, service organizations, and public schools. She divides her time between the Pacific NW, Dawson City, Yukon, and Skagway, AK, where several times she's been named Tour Guide of the Month by Princess Cruise Lines.

She is the mother of three and grandmother of seven.

Brenda Wilbee